Born in West London, Paul French first sought military adventure in the County of London Yeomanry and then 21 SAS (V). Here, Paul discovered a yearning for hard work and arduous duty. A subsequent defence contract took him to Abu Dhabi where he learnt of Rhodesia and its attractions. Holidaying in Rhodesia, Paul took the opportunity to join the Rhodesian Army, serving with the renowned Rhodesian SAS and Selous Scouts. In 1980, Paul moved to the South African Defence Force, joining its elite 6 Reconnaissance Commando. Upon leaving the SADF a career in private security followed. An accomplished skydiver, Paul has thousands of jumps to his credit, and still jumps today. Married to Petah, Paul has three children. He continues to work in the security industry and now lives in the south-west of England. *Shadows of A Forgotten Past* is his first book.

SHADOWS OF A FORGOTTEN PAST

To the edge with the Rhodesian SAS and Selous Scouts

Paul French

Helion & Company

G G Books UK

Co-published in 2012 by:
Helion & Company Limited
26 Willow Road
Solihull
West Midlands
B91 1UE
England
Tel. 0121 705 3393
Fax 0121 711 4075
Email: info@helion.co.uk
Website: www.helion.co.uk

and

GG Books UK
Rugby
Warwickshire
Tel. 07921 709307
Website: www.30degreessouth.co.uk

Reprinted 2016
Designed and typeset by Farr out Publications, Wokingham, Berkshire
Cover designed by Euan Carter, Leicester (www.euancarter.com)
Printed by Hobbs The Printers Ltd, Totton, Hampshire

Text © Paul French 2012
Photographs © Paul French unless otherwise noted
Maps © GG Books/Helion & Company Ltd

ISBN 978-1-908916-60-0

British Library Cataloguing-in-Publication Data.
A catalogue record for this book is available from the British Library.

All rights reserved. No part of this publication may be reproduced, stored in a retrieval system,or transmitted, in any form, or by any means, electronic, mechanical, photocopying, recording or otherwise, without the express written consent of Helion & Company Limited and GG Books.

For details of other military history titles published by Helion & Company Limited contact the above address, or visit our website: http://www.helion.co.uk.

We always welcome receiving book proposals from prospective authors.

Contents

List of photographs	6
List of maps	10
Author's note	11
Glossary of terms and abbreviations	13
Introduction	16
1. Selection comparisons	23
2. Rhodesian SAS	33
3. Selous Scouts Pseudo Operations	48
4. The operation that went wrong	59
5. Anecdotes	73
6. Raid on Joshua Nkomo, Lusaka, 14 April 1979	103
7. The operation that went right	108
8. Operation Tepid, October 1979	141
9. The Cisco and Marianne Guerreiro story	146
10. Mozambique National Resistance	156
11. End of an era	177
12. Angola, Somalia and Iraq	181
Appendix: Warning signs	201

List of photographs

The 1970 21 SAS Canoe Club Devizes–Westminster canoe race, 120 miles non-stop. The author is in the front cockpit. *Photo* Harry Matthews — 19

21 SAS kitting up for a para drop in Europe from US Air Force C-47 Skytrain. Facing the camera is the author (left) and Harry Matthews (right). *Photo* Harry Matthews — 20

Preparing for a parachute deployment. *Photo* Jake Harper-Ronald — 35

Camp attack. *Private collection* — 39

Camp attack. *Private collection* — 40

1976 Elim Mission base camp, 1976, after the long walk back from Chioco. The author (left) and Jake Harper-Ronald. — 41

Mavue Camp, 1976. From left: Jake Harper-Ronald, Bob Pike and the author. — 42

Mavue Camp, 1976. Clearing out the ZANLA camp. — 42

Mavue Camp, 1976. A view from a building. — 43

Mavue Camp, 1976. An ammo truck goes up after Vampire strike. — 44

Return from Mavue, 1976. Pushing trucks out of the sand again. — 45

C Squadron 1 Rhodesian SAS, Kabrit barracks, Salisbury, Rhodesia, March 1980. — 47

ZANLA terrorists training in Mozambique. *Photos* Dennis Croukamp — 52

Two pages from a ZANLA terrorist's notebook. *Photos* Dennis Croukamp — 54

Female ZANLA terrorists training in Mozambique. *Photo* Dennis Croukamp — 56

Building the first 'Pig' armoured personnel carrier, Selous Scouts MT workshop. *Photo* Dennis Croukamp — 61

Selous Scouts 'Pig' armoured car on Mercedes Unimog chassis. *Photo* Dennis Croukamp — 61

Two images of a Selous Scouts vehicle column on the march. *Photos* Dennis Croukamp — 62

View across Rio Savi at Masangena in Mozambique. Selous Scouts troops attack the ZANLA camp on opposite side. — 65

A 'Pig' in Mozambique, 1976. *Photo* Dennis Croukamp — 65

The author on a railway line in Mozambique. 1976. *Photo* Dennis Croukamp — 67

Blown rail line, 1976. *Photo* Dennis Croukamp — 68

LIST OF PHOTOGRAPHS

Selous Scouts Mercedes Unimog 2.5 truck, 1976. *Photo* Dennis Croukamp	70
Selous Scouts column gets a visit from 7 Squadron RhAF. *Photo* Dennis Croukamp	70
Charlie Small (Rhodesian Engineers). *Photo* Dennis Croukamp	80
Author with Magirus Deutz truck in South Africa before deployment into Mozambique, 1980.	84
The rear of my Magirus Deutz truck. Before deployment into Mozambique, 1980.	84
Chambeshi bridges from Canberra photo recon. *Photo* RhAF	110
Author in free-fall over Salisbury Rhodesia. *Camera* Dennis Croukamp	113
Author front extreme right, PJI Mike Witshire seated centre. *Photo* RhAF	115
Jack Malloch's Spitfire Mk2I. *Private collection*	122
Chambeshi rail bridge after the operation. Photo *Rhodesia Herald*	139
Cisco and Marianne at home. 2007.	146
Cisco in the SAS, the first time. *Photo* Cisco Guerreiro	148
Author with Cisco Guerreiro in his 'local', 2007.	151
Marianne Guerreiro with her Rhodesian Signals Corps troop, 1976. *Photo* Marianne Guerreiro	152
Marianne receives the Southern Cross medal from General Viljoen, 1985. *Photo* Marianne Guerreiro	154
Marianne Guerreiro with her South African uniform and medals, 2007.	154
Andrea Matsangaise. *Photo* Cisco Guerreiro	157
Frelimo soldiers pose for the camera before going on operations. *Photo* author's collection	158
Frelimo soldiers	159
Frelimo soldiers	160
Luke Mhlanga with captured Chinese 82mm mortar, 1979.	161
The team with Luke Mhangla and MNR commanders, 1979.	162
MNR troops parade following air resupply, 1979.	164
Captured Frelimo soldier in Luke's base camp, 1979.	166
Captured 82mm mortar in Luke Mhlanga's base camp, 1979.	166
Frelimo revolutionary poem.	168
Author with 82mm mortar in MNR base camp, 1979.	171
MNR commanders.	174
Cash in transit, at Box Gafar, the cigarette seller, Luanda, 1993.	184
Guards on parade in Luanda before the new uniforms arrived, 1993.	185
Guards with new uniforms at the new parade area, Luanda, 1993.	185

Train Hard, Fight Easy. Angolan Air Force Parachute School, Luanda 1993. 187
Baghdad, Iraq, June 2003. The author on throne in Saddam
    Hussein's palace. 193
Letter of appreciation, Chief of Staff Task Force Olympia. 198
Al Hadr ruins, 80 kilometres west of Q-West airfield. 199

Colour section photographs

Rhodesian National Parachute Championships, 1975. Back from
    left: Boss Douglas (RhAF), Kevin Milligan (RhAF), Paul
    Hogan (RhAF), J.C. Grey (SAS), Mike Wiltshire (RhAF).
    Front from left: J. Hurly (RhAF), J. Lang (SAS) and the author.
Author's Rhodesian SAS Parachute Log book.
SAS Log Book entry: Operational Jump – 15/01/79 – static line into Zambia
SAS Log Book entries: Operational Jump – 09/06/79 – static line
    into Mozambique; Operational Jump – 07/07/79 – static line
    into Mozambique; Operational Jump – 4/10/79 – Freefall into
    Zambia – Operation Cheese
Author's Selous Scout Parachute logbook
Selous Scouts Log Book entry: Operational Jump – 24/10/76 –
    freefall into Mozambique
6 Troop Selous Scouts in a base camp preparing dinner.
Cpl Frank Ephraim of 6 Troop Selous Scouts walking off the drop zone.
6 Troop Selous Scouts para-trained element, 1977. The author is sixth from left.
1978, the new Bell Huey helicopters at New Sarum. The author is
    second from right.
Cleaning a 76mm recoilless rifle.
Raid on Joshua Nkomo 1979 – the ferry *Sea Lion* in transit on Lake Kariba.
Raid on Joshua Nkomo 1979 – Land Rovers on board the *Sea Lion*.
Raid on Joshua Nkomo 1979 – Andy Anderson standing on rear of Land Rover.
Raid on Joshua Nkomo 1979 – The Land Rover that broke down.
Raid on Joshua Nkomo 1979 – The author's Land Rover. The
    author is on the front machine gun and Cpl Anton Grobler is
    standing at back.
Grand Reef airfield, 1979. A call-sign waits for a helicopter before
    deploying to Mozambique.

LIST OF PHOTOGRAPHS

A ZANLA camp in Mozambique, 1979. Jimmy Ramsay about to enter a bunker. *Photo* author's collection
Kabrit barracks, 1979. A Huey helicopter returns a call sign after a deployment.
Chipinga, 10 June 1979. C Squadron returned from a road ambush in Mozambique. Author is at extreme right.
Security force patrols during the election in Salisbury, March 1980.
Mr and Mrs French after the wedding, 21 March 1980.
The wedding party. From left: Pete and Trish Leonard, Frank Kaszas, Di Squairs, the author and Mrs French, Doug Parker.
Rhodesian SAS 106mm recoilless rifles at Inkomo range, 1980.
6 Recce Commando training jump at Duku Duku, Zululand, 1980.
Rear L-R: Rhodesian camo shirt with sergeant's stripes, SAS camo shirt wings, Selous Scout beret, British SAS beret, South African Reconnaissance Commando beret, Rhodesian camo shirt with sergeant's stripes and Scouts camo shirt wings.
Centre L-R: Selous Scouts operator's wings, Rhodesian infantry combat badge.
Front L-R : British SAS stable belt, medals, Selous Scout stable belt.
50th anniversary of the SAS. Free-fallers, Johannesburg, 1991.
50th anniversary of the SAS. All jumpers and the DC-3, Johannesburg, 1991.
Angolan Air Force Mi8 helicopter with parachute display team, Luanda, 1993.
Angolan Air Force Parachute School, Luanda, 1993. From left: Tenente Francisco and Capitão Diamante.
UN compound, Mogadishu, Somalia, 1994.
Mogadishu from the air, UN compound in foreground.
Author with Nepalese security personnel, Iraq, 2005.
Mosul, 2004, Eugene Pomeroy with repaired vehicle following IED blast.
Call sign 30C, Mosul, Iraq, 2004. Eugene Pomeroy kneeling at left, author kneeling centre.
Author with Fijian security personnel.
Tools of the trade, Q-West airfield, Iraq 2004/5.
Skydive Dubai, February 2012, the author at extreme left. *Photo* Pete Marsden

List of maps

In colour section

Rhodesia and Mozambique
Iraq and Kurdistan
Mosul City, Iraq

Author's note

This book was originally intended solely for my family and not for publication. However, as the manuscript progressed, it appeared that it might prove of interest to the general reader, particularly followers of military memoirs. Members of my family have served in most of the conflicts that the British army was involved in during the twentieth century and some in the nineteenth century. Sadly, their stories of colonial wars, world wars and the retreat from Empire were never committed to paper: their stories are lost forever.

There are many books on the market that cover events in Africa and the Middle East of the past fifty years, the devious actions of politicians and the tactics, strategies and weapons involved in the plethora of insurgencies that have beset the region following the end of the Second World War. However, there are few books that describe the life of the ordinary foot soldier: how he lived, what he ate, how he trained, what the bush was like, how he amused himself, how he reacted to the deaths of close friends and why he was there. This book fills that gap to some extent.

I am fortunate that I started recording an outline of my military career during the 1980s, not long after some of the events described and before memories became too dulled with time, but there may well be errors in dates, times, places and names; for this the blame is mine alone.

Everything mentioned in this book happened to me or happened when I was there or was told to me by those who were there. The Guerreiros took me into their confidence at their house in the Algarve and I wrote down their words verbatim; they are people of few words and so their personal memories are very special. Dennis Croukamp related some of his adventures to me and I retell them here. Kevin Milligan tells, in his own words, the story of parachuting operations from the perspective of a Rhodesian Air Force Parachute Operations Officer. His job was to ensure that the paratroopers and all their kit were delivered intact to the right location at the right time. He achieved this time and time again. His story has not been told before and is therefore unique.

After the conflicts in sub-Saharan Africa of the 1970s and 1980s, my story continues with civilian security work in Africa in the 1990s and into the early years of the twenty-first century with a private military company in Iraq.

With time, attitudes change and public perception of what is right and what is wrong also changes. The way events have unfolded in southern Africa and elsewhere over the past fifty years has proved that we were right in doing what we did. I hope future generations see this and enjoy my story.

After all have come and gone
We will remain shadows of a forgotten past
Those that follow
After we are long forgotten
Will say:
Here stayed men of substance
Therefore I pray
God bless all sons of Rhodesia
At least we tried, did we not?
Yet how did we fail
When we were so sincere?

Glossary of terms and abbreviations

AK-47	Assault rifle of Soviet origin
AS	African Soldier
AWOL	absent without leave
baobab	large tree indigenous to southern Africa bushveld
basha	soldier's temporary shelter
Big Means	HF radio
BSAP	British South Africa Police, Rhodesia's police force
bundu	remote bush area
claymore	anti-personnel mine, remotely detonated
cordtex	Thin plastic sleeve containing TNT explosive, looks like washing line, and detonates at 22,000 feet per second
CTT	combat tracker team
DZ	drop zone, parachutists
FNLA	*Frente Nacional de Libertação de Angola*, National Front for the Liberation of Angola, headed by Holden Roberto
ES	European Soldiers, applied to all white soldiers
FPLM	*Forças Populares de Libertação de Moçambique*, military wing of Frelimo
FUT	follow-up troops
frantan	locally made napalm
Frelimo	*Frente de Libertação de Moçambique*, Front for the Liberation of Mozambique, headed by Samora Machel
gook	communist terrorist
HALO	freefall parachuting: High Altitude Low Opening
Head Shed	headquarters. An SAS term, because their headquarters were often located in temporary structures
HF	high frequency, radio
IED	Improvised Explosive Device
jack in	to give up, concede defeat
LZ	landing zone, helicopters

Log PT	group physical exercise using a tree, or telegraph pole
LUP	laying-up position
MAG	Belt-fed 7.62mm machine gun of Belgian origin
murungu	white man
mushonga	a magic potion, concocted by a *nanga*, or traditional healer, to provide luck in love or gambling or immunity to bullets
MNR	Mozambique National Resistance, *also* Renamo (*Resistência Nacional Moçambicana*)
NCO	non-commissioned officer, lance-corporal, corporal, sergeant, warrant officer, etc.
ND	negligent discharge, of firearm
OP	observation post
PC	Political Commissar
PJI	Parachute Jumping Instructor
PT	physical training
PTS	Parachute Training School
RAR	Rhodesian African Rifles
RhAF	Rhodesian Air Force
RLI	Rhodesian Light Infantry
RSM	Regimental Sergeant-Major, senior NCO in a battalion
RTU	return to unit
RV	rendezvous
SAS	Special Air Service
sitrep	situation report
Small Means	VHF radio
SOP	Standard Operating Procedure
Special Branch	A branch of the BSAP specializing in intelligence gathering
SSM	Squadron Sergeant-Major, the senior NCO in a squadron
SKS	semi-automatic assault rifle of communist origin
tambu	rope made from tree bark
troopie	trooper or private soldier
TA	Territorial Army, UK Army Reserve
TF	Territorial Force, Rhodesian Army Reserve
TNT	trinitrotoluene, explosive
TT	turned terrorist
TTL	Tribal Trust Land, reserved for Africans only

GLOSSARY OF TERMS AND ABBREVIATIONS

'turn over'	a bookmaker on a race-course would stand on a box and shout the odds he was offering to attract 'mug punters' as the bookies call their clients. If protection money had not been paid to the gang 'running' that course then the bookie's box, and the bookie, would be turned over, and the bookie was out of business. If the bookie was very unlucky, he would be beaten up, razored with a cut-throat razor or both.
VHF	very high frequency, radio
ZAPU	Zimbabwe African People's Union, backed by the Soviet Union and headed by Joshua Nkomo
ZIPRA	Zimbabwe People's Revolutionary Army, military wing of ZAPU
ZANU	Zimbabwe African National Union, backed by Red China and headed by Robert Mugabe
ZANLA	Zimbabwe African National Liberation Army, military wing of ZANU

Introduction

In the beginning ... and a bit more

We are all in the gutter
But some of us are looking at the stars
Oscar Wilde

My earliest, vivid recollection is standing outside Hounslow police station in Middlesex, west London, in about 1950 when I would have been three years old. Everybody seemed so very tall then but they probably weren't. My father was bailing out one of his 'runners'. My father was a bookie's clerk working for a bookmaker operating out of premises over a shop near the Hounslow bus station. The 'runner' collected betting slips in the area from shops, offices, factories and the like. They were called runners because they used to have to run from the police. I think my father enjoyed life as a bookie on the racecourse and on the street. He once told me about the protection rackets on the racecourses, of the 'bucket money' that bookies had to pay to the old man with the bucket to wet their sponges. If they didn't pay then they got 'turned over' by the gang running the protection racket. In those days they used coshes and cut-throat razors. The bookmaker my dad had worked for in the 1930s and '40s died in the early '50s and so Dad then worked for other bookies including William Hill in London. In 1959 betting shops were legalized which spelled the demise of street bookies and runners. In 1959 Dad's pal, David Capel, opened a betting shop in Harlesden in north-west London and my dad ran it. It was a licence to print money in those days. As the years wore on the market became saturated and government taxation has made it much less profitable.

Mother told me he had a hard life as a kid. His family lived at the top end of Portobello Road in Ladbroke Grove, west London. He was one of ten children of whom two died young. When he was ten, my mother said, before school in the morning he used to run to a house in Kensington, owned by a retired army captain and light the fires. His wage was his breakfast. There was no depression in the 1930s, my father said, because things had always been like that.

My father was conscripted in 1940 and served as an infantryman during the Second World War. I believe he enjoyed his experiences. Many of his friends in the 9th Battalion Bedfordshire & Hertfordshire Regiment were killed paddling across the Rhine in 1944, whilst using folding boats made from canvas and plywood. I am glad to say he missed that operation or I might not be here now. At the war's end he struggled to understand why he had been conscripted in 1940 to free Poland from the Fascists, only to have the politicians hand it over to the Communists in 1945.

My paternal grandfather, Joe French, was a painter and decorator and served in the First World War. I still have his three pay books. He enlisted first on 11th November 1914 at Shepherds Bush, west London, in the 15th Battalion, Royal Fusiliers but was discharged on 29th January 1915 as medically unfit. He enlisted again on 14th December 1915 in the 5th Battalion London Fusiliers but was again discharged on medical grounds. His third enlistment in 1917 into the Royal Engineers was successful as manpower was drying up and recruiters were becoming less fussy. Many working-class men a century ago were unfit for military service due to poor diet, disease and poor living conditions. Joe French's eldest brother, and there were thirteen children in that family, won the Military Medal at Cambrai in 1917 while serving in the 15th Battalion London Regiment. Sadly, he was killed in 1918.

Joe's father was a gardener whose brother, John George French, was a soldier for twenty-two years. He enlisted at eighteen in 1859 at Westminster and was posted to B Company, 24th Regiment of Foot in Brecon. He saw service in the Indian Ocean, Cape Colony and Natal in the Zulu War of 1879. He was at the defence of Rorke's Drift. I have his discharge papers and it is interesting to see that he received his third stripe on 22 January, the day Rorke's Drift was relieved. However, he lost the stripe in June of that year, eventually retiring as a private soldier.

My maternal grandfather, Pat Sullivan, an immigrant of Irish stock, was a labourer with Marylebone Borough Council in West London. He also served in the First World War. After being gassed on the Western Front, he spent a few months in Dublin and the rest of the war on garrison duty in Malta. He took the family post office savings book with him to Malta, and on his returned to London at the end of the war, the savings book was empty. Interestingly, my parents holidayed in Malta in the early 1960s and hired a taxi driven by a Maltese called Pat Sullivan whose father had been a soldier during the First World War. Soldiers will always do what soldiers always do.

In the 1950s my brother Tony, eight years my senior, joined the British Army. At the time this seemed to me like a big adventure. He passed out of the Royal Military Academy Sandhurst after officer training and gained an engineering degree from Cambridge University. He was commissioned into the Royal Electrical and Mechanical Engineers and reached the rank of captain. He served in Aden during the retreat from Empire but served most of his time in Germany. He was bored, I think, and resigned after ten years' service.

I joined the Army Cadets in Wembley when I was thirteen and had some good times. I used to enjoy running and walking and we did plenty of it. I had two good friends at school, Alan Newbold and Colin Hartley, and we were all in the cadets together, where we enjoyed the adventures of camping and shooting. Colin joined the Army Air Corps as an air mechanic after an apprenticeship at Glacier Bearings in Alperton where his father worked. Alan worked for his father as a painter and decorator.

After I finished school, I became a draughtsman in north-west London. It was mundane from the outset but at that time there was not much else on offer. When I turned eighteen, I joined the County of London Yeomanry, a Territorial Army (TA) unit, and drove Land Rovers and Ferret armoured cars. However, the unit did not offer the adventure I was looking for and I was not overly upset when it was closed down in 1967, as a part of government defence cuts enacted by the appropriately named Generals Hackett and Carver.

In 1968 I joined another TA unit, 21 SAS, at the Duke of York's HQ in Chelsea. This was more like it. I did the selection course, it was challenging and I enjoyed it. I 'buddied' up with three other young men: Evan Parsons, Doug Parker and Harry Mathews. Evan stayed on in the TA and eventually became 2 i/c of 21 SAS and worked in airline security. Doug later went to Africa with his wife Theresa, where he worked as a civilian, first in Rhodesia and then in South Africa where they still live. Harry stayed on in the TA for several years. After working as a photographer for the *Surrey Comet*, he joined MI5 in 1970 when the organization was expanding due to the increased Soviet presence in London. He worked for MI5 for fourteen years before joining 14 Intelligence Company (later to become the Special Reconnaissance Regiment). He completed two two-year tours in Northern Ireland in the 1980s and was twice Mentioned in Dispatches.

At 21 SAS we were trained extensively. Everybody did a static-line parachute course and a demolition course. We learned a wide variety of military skills. At the time our sister unit, 22 SAS, was committed to Oman and a lot of

The 1970 21 SAS Canoe Club Devizes–Westminster canoe race, 120 miles non-stop. The author is in the front cockpit. *Photo* Harry Matthews

the NATO exercises they would have otherwise undertaken in Europe were allocated to us. Exercises included at least two trips a year to Denmark, several to Germany and others to Belgium and Holland, as well as covering the UK in a wide variety of destinations.

One exciting event was the Devizes–Westminster canoe race in 1970. 21 SAS Regiment entered four two-man canoes and we won the team trophy against some stiff competition from the Parachute Regiment and the Royal Marines. Harry and I completed a free-fall course in 1971, which I enjoyed but I don't think Harry did. I skydive to this day but Harry never did another skydive as far as I know.

The number of training days available to us was virtually unlimited and I took full advantage of this. I gave up my civilian job in 1970 to do courses and exercises with 21 SAS all over Europe. After one fifteen-month period of almost full-time TA employment, I was able to buy a new Mini Cooper for cash. These were good days. However, the regiment's primary role in Germany, still classified, was as adventurous as train-spotting and I could not take it seriously. Coupled with the tedium of drawing office work, I was getting bored. I felt I needed a change, so I started looking for jobs overseas. My first overseas contract was with Airwork Services as a missile fitter on contract to the Abu

Dhabi Defence Force Air Wing from 1972 to 1974. It was tremendously tedious but I stuck it out and put some money in the bank.

During my time at Airwork Services, a new man appeared on the contract who had previously worked on the Airwork contract in Rhodesia doing overhauls and inspections on Rhodesian Air Force aircraft. He described some of the attractions of the country—Victoria Falls, Lake Kariba and Inyanga—and it sounded very appealing. I made up my mind to visit the country on holiday. On completion of my time in Abu Dhabi, I went home to London and bought a thirty-day ticket to Salisbury, Rhodesia in February 1974.

I can remember arriving at Salisbury International. It was small and quaint and very clean; in fact, the whole town was spotless. I quickly settled in and was offered a job within a week of being in the country. I remember waking up one Sunday morning in my hotel with a feeling I had forgotten something. After checking my ticket, I realized my return flight to UK had left the night before. It was time to get a job. I started work with Johnson & Fletcher Air Conditioning in Salisbury at the end of February 1974.

I found the skydiving club – and the way it was run – like a breath of fresh air after the restrictions of the UK clubs who seemed to have lost sight of the fact that they were a service industry. Life was good and I was really enjoying myself. In the first few weeks I made plenty of friends and went on several trips

21 SAS kitting up for a para drop in Europe from US Air Force C-47 Skytrain. Facing the camera is the author (left) and Harry Matthews (right). *Photo* Harry Matthews

to the tourist spots of Inyanga and Kariba. After a short while, I became friends with other skydivers who were serving in the army and, as a result, enlisted in the Rhodesian army on a three-year contract. The tales of my service in the Rhodesian SAS and the Selous Scouts are recounted later in this book.

In 1977, at the end of my first contract with the Rhodesian army, I went to Durban, South Africa, to 1 Reconnaissance Commando and enquired about joining the Recces. I was pointed in the direction of General Loots in Pretoria who interviewed me and arranged for me to visit the Military Medical Institute in Pretoria for a rigorous three-day medical and psychological examination. I was subsequently offered the rank of corporal in 1 Recce Commando, however I returned to Rhodesia to give the offer some thought and instead re-joined the Rhodesian army. I intended to see the Rhodesian war through to its conclusion.

I met my wife in 1977 at the Zimbabwe Ruins, now Great Zimbabwe, and married Petah Holliday in the District Commissioner's office in Salisbury on 21 March 1980. We left Rhodesia when Robert Mugabe came to power, to begin a new life in South Africa, departing Salisbury in our VW Beetle with everything we owned, including the cat, and travelled to Durban. Mugabe's regime had earlier threatened to hold war-crime tribunals for Selous Scouts soldiers so I thought I had no choice but to leave. In Pretoria I signed on with the South African Recce Commandos to serve with 6 Recce in Durban.

Our first child, Anthony, arrived in 1981, then Mathew came along in 1983 and Emma the following year. We initially struggled for money and I had to resign from the South African army in 1982 because it was so badly paid. I also felt I was being used by a political machine whose ideology I did not believe in. The big money at that time was in Johannesburg and we moved there in 1983. I worked for a number of companies in Johannesburg before taking up a position in Angola in the early 1990s.

The Angolan job paid in US dollars and enabled me to get my family out of South Africa shortly before Mandela's regime came to power. I was concerned that all the bright hopes for a new South Africa would not last long and that the regime following Mandela would be far more corrupt than the whites had been. It was important to get my children out of the country and back to the UK so that they could adapt to their new environment while still of school-going age.

After a number of UK and overseas contract jobs in Indonesia, Saudi Arabia, Tanzania, Kenya, Nigeria and trips to places like Somalia, I worked in Iraq from 2003 to 2006. Life has been varied; currently it is good and getting better. Our eldest son is in the British army and so is our daughter. Our middle child is in manufacturing. My wife and I frequently travel on overseas holidays and we love every minute of them.

Life is good.

1
Selection comparisons

I successfully completed Territorial SAS Selection in the UK in 1968, and I passed the Rhodesian SAS and Rhodesian Selous Scout selections in the 1970s. As mentioned, before joining the South African Defence Force, I underwent three days of psychological and physical testing before being posted to the South African Reconnaissance Commandos. These are my thoughts on how the various selections and assessments compared.

My first Squadron Sergeant-Major (SSM) in 21 SAS was John Davies, a big man with a West Country accent and a large moustache. Being too young, he had missed out on the Second World War, but enlisted shortly thereafter in the Malayan Scouts and served in B Squadron. He became a founder member of 22 SAS when the Malayan Scouts was rebadged as SAS. He never did a selection course: the Malayan Scouts took volunteers, put them through a jungle training course and then into a squadron. If they liked the man they kept him and if he didn't shape up, he was Returned To Unit (RTU'd). Selection courses proper really only began after 22 SAS returned from the Far East in 1958, he said. John had reservations about the validity of selection courses, believing the best way to find out about people and to assess them was to work alongside them.

Once, in a pub over a few drinks, I received a 'lecture' from an old 22 SAS hand. He described the way in which selections had developed over the years. Initially, he said, the men were met at a railway station, where they were given a rucksack, map, compass and a ration pack. Then they got on to a truck and after being driven to the exercise area, they started walking. The pass rate was only about five per cent. Something had to be done, he said, about this high wastage rate. The 'Head Shed' at Hereford—the 22 SAS command—had a big think about how to reduce the wastage rate. It was decided to give the men a few days in barracks in Hereford to learn basic map-reading and to become accustomed to the equipment they would be using. The pass rate barely improved. The next idea was to put all the recruits through a two-week 'pre-selection' course, comprising map-reading and basic fitness training. Still the pass rate stayed low and I understand they are still around five per cent. There must be a lesson in all this.

The British SAS selection course

I will start with the TA SAS course that I did in October 1968. So much has been written about the British SAS selection course over the years that I won't bore the reader with too many of the finer details. The course began with two days of 'sickeners'; exercises in which the recruits were put through demoralizing and pointless routines, carried out in groups. This was followed by Test Week, which consisted of five days of long, arduous walks with heavy rucksacks in the Brecon Beacons in all weathers, done on an individual basis. The first three days were checkpoint-to-checkpoint walks, with a speed march on day four and a 'long drag', or endurance march, on day five. The wastage rate was high.

Interestingly, a man had died on selection a year or so before I did my course. Owing to the camouflaged kit he was wearing and the fact he had wandered off the beaten track, finding his body proved difficult. Because of this, my course was issued with white anoraks which we were sternly warned to wear at all times. Those of you with military experience might have guessed by now that it snowed during Test Week that October and we still had to wear our white anoraks!

On my course we were issued with Far East ration packs which comprised a handful of rice, a tin of sardines, biscuits, a compressed dehydrated block of meat and two teabags. Such rations are entirely unsuitable for arduous physical labour in a cold climate. Our rucksacks were of Second World War vintage and hideously uncomfortable. By modern standards, our equipment and rations were wholly inadequate.

The Rhodesian SAS selection course

During the Malayan Scouts period of the late 1940s, C Squadron Malayan Scouts comprised volunteers from Rhodesia. When the unit was rebadged as 22 Special Air Service Regiment in 1951, C Squadron remained Rhodesian. On disbandment the Rhodesians went home, but the name C Squadron was retained on the 22 SAS Order Of Battle, where it remains to this day. In 1961 the Rhodesian Army revived C Squadron, which was to retain strong links with Hereford and 22 SAS for the next two decades, despite the 1965 unilateral declaration of independence (UDI) by Rhodesia which acrimoniously severed links with the Crown and served as a pre-cursor to the Rhodesian bush war.

The Rhodesian SAS selection was only slightly different to the British course because the people who designed the course had completed their selections in the UK. At the time, i.e. pre-1965, with Rhodesia a British colony, many Rhodesian servicemen undertook training courses in Britain.

On a Friday morning in early 1974 we volunteers assembled at Cranborne barracks in Salisbury, Rhodesia. There were men from the UK, France, Canada, USA, Australia, South Africa, New Zealand and Rhodesia. The foreigners were mostly former regular soldiers; the Rhodesians were serving regulars from other Rhodesian units, with no national servicemen involved. After a parade, kit was issued which included FN rifles, magazines, ammunition, sleeping bags, mess tins and cooking gear. Friday passed in a leisurely fashion and we got to know each other.

Then it all changed on Friday evening.

For the next forty-eight hours we were running, swimming, doing log PT and generally getting extremely tired with little rest. The log PT consisted of team races, with each team carrying a telegraph pole around the local neighbourhood. The only 'meal' we enjoyed was one cup of cold black tea and two slices of stale bread. Sleep was limited to perhaps four hours over the whole period and some of the volunteers 'jacked in'.

When the forty-eight hours were up, it was a relief to clamber onto the four waiting trucks and travel east to the Inyanga mountains in the northeast of the country near the Mozambican border. We had six hours' uninterrupted sleep on the journey even though we were packed in like sardines. On arrival at Inyanga, we were each issued with a map, one ration pack and four blue-painted house bricks plus one log between eight men. Rucksacks were weighed to ensure everyone was carrying the minimum weight of forty-five pounds. The Squadron Sergeant-Major (SSM) of C Squadron, was nicknamed was 'Snake'; he called the bricks 'pies' and suffice to say, we thought he had a very strange sense of humour.

Day 1 was a team log race across country. This was a bit like orienteering but with logs, rucksacks and rifles. It was a good eight-hour march and some people did not get in by the cut-off time in the afternoon and were immediately RTU'd. We slept together as a group that night and feasted on the ration packs which were adequate. Although it was winter, for me the days were relatively warm, the nights cool and the scenery magnificent. While the terrain was undulating, it was not severe. I was beginning to enjoy the course.

Day 2 began with each person being issued with one ration pack and a map reference. Rucksacks were inspected to ensure we had not lost any 'pies'. Men were set off individually to make their way to the next rendezvous point. We were not told what the cut-off time was and were warned not to walk in groups or on roads for fear of being RTU'd. The terrain this day was more mountainous, with thick vegetation in places and a lot of walking across the grain of the country. It proved disastrous for me. I got into some very thick bush and was lost much of the time. An Australian told me that the bush he got tangled in at Inyanga was every bit as thick as the jungle in Papua New Guinea where he had done his jungle training course with the Australian SAS. Most of us made the RV in time and again we slept together as a group. A few more people had dropped out.

Day 3 began in the usual way. We were each issued with a ration pack, had our rucksacks weighed and inspected for 'pies' and were given a map reference. Squadron Sergeant-Major 'Snake' spoiled things for some of the men by adding a few extra bricks to those who had lost theirs or who had been spotted walking in pairs, in groups or on roads. The RV was on top of a mountain called World's View. It was a tiring day's walk but the weather was cool, the views were exhilarating and I really enjoyed it. One can almost see forever from World's View. Again, we slept that night as a group.

Day 4 dawned misty and very cool. This was speed-march day, which involved racing to the top of a large mountain, immediately turning around, coming down and then traversing the length of a long valley. It was an individual march and, again, we lost some of our volunteers along the way.

Day 5 was 'Long Drag' day. Beginning at dawn, this was a very long endurance march, done individually. There was a cut-off time and once again we lost a few more people.

The next day, the survivors were trucked back to Salisbury to prepare for continuation training the following Monday. This course had a relatively high pass rate of around ten per cent mainly, I believe, due to the fact that everyone who passed had previous regular or territorial service. Overall, I can say that I thoroughly enjoyed the Rhodesian selection. The weather was superb, the scenery was awesome and I made many good friends. Those who survived the course became friends for life and I look back on it as a thoroughly enjoyable 'walking holiday', even though I had some huge blood blisters on my feet and the rucksack had worn sores on my hips.

The Selous Scouts Selection Course

This selection course was different to others I had done, and was significantly harder. Selous Scout selection courses lasted approximately thirty days and were held at one of several camps in the Zambezi valley in the general vicinity of Kariba dam. My course, which I did in September 1976, was typical. At the beginning of the course 200 African soldiers (AS, i.e. black) and forty European soldiers (ES, i.e. white), both regular and territorial, were trucked from Salisbury to Camp Mushonga (Camp 'Magic Potion') approximately twenty kilometres from Kariba township. The ES contingent included five soldiers from C Squadron. The other white soldiers came from units such as the Rhodesian Light Infantry (RLI), the Rhodesia Regiment (RR) and from units as the Rhodesian Corps of Signals and the Rhodesian Army Medical Corps. Near Camp Mushonga, on the edge of Lake Kariba, the Selous Scouts had a tracking school called Camp Wafa Wafa Wasara Wasara ('Look out, look out, you're dead, you're dead') and another camp some distance away called Camp Baobab. All those on the course, both AS and ES, had rucksacks or full-service marching order, FN rifles, one magazine each and sleeping bags.

I had been briefed by two friends who previously had failed the course, so I had a stash of dried food and two gas cigarette lighters (not available in Rhodesia) hidden in my kit. On arrival at Camp Mushonga, we were all paraded and searched. My food was taken off me but they did not find the lighters. The first briefing involved being told that everyone was equal and that each ES had to buddy up with an AS. (At the time, there was racial segregation in Rhodesia, even in the military.) We were then divided into four groups and allocated different areas of the camp. Each group comprised about fifty black and ten white soldiers.

Day 1 and we set about making shelters with poles and grass collected locally. The black soldier I buddied up with was a decent chap with a fair command of English. No food was issued that day. After our shelters, or *bashas*, were erected, we did PT until dark. We then had to sit around a fire and learn songs in chiShona, the most widely spoken ethnic language of the country. Most of the AS were from eastern and central Rhodesia and were chiShona speakers. A small number were from western Rhodesia and spoke Sindebele, a Zulu dialect. Well after midnight we were instructed that each group had to put out a guard until dawn. The problem was that black soldiers generally did not have watches. After I had inserted my watch into a clear plastic bag with many complicated knots, a guard roster was made out and the watch bag was tied to a tree. By dawn it was apparent the guard roster had been a disaster. The watch was out of the bag and had been wound on by several hours. Lesson learned: do not trust anybody.

Day 2 started with a dawn road run, then PT for an hour. After that, we were allowed an hour to wash and sweep our group areas before parade. Again no food was issued, although the instructors, particularly Charlie Krause, would walk around chewing on T-bone steaks, muttering, "Shit steak, that one." Then we were introduced to the ropes course. This was the longest ropes course I have ever seen. Ropes were vertical, horizontal, inclined, and with nets and poles for walking over deep pits. There were no safety features. After a couple of times around the course we were treated to a bush survival lecture by Sergeant Zingai, an instructor from the nearby tracking school. The only thing to eat in the bush at that time of year, before the rains, was *ndarari*, a spinach-like plant that tasted vile. I filled up on water.

That night we had more singing until the small hours and the white soldiers had to present vignettes on their life histories. By the end of the day, there was a lot of whingeing about the lack of food from some of the ES personnel, even from two of the C Squadron men which surprised me; one was a former Royal Marine and the other former Australian SAS.

Day 3 began, as usual, with road running and PT, before a swim in the lake. After the swim and sweeping of group areas we were assembled … for a surprise. There was to be a group ropes-course competition, with a prize of a pint of sour milk and half a loaf of stale bread for each buddy pair. Highly motivated, our group won the competition. We had to eat and drink our prize on the spot; the milk and bread disappeared in a blur in case 'they' (meaning Charlie Krause and the other instructors) decided to take it away. There was a lot of complaining from those who didn't get any, but we were not allowed to share with other groups.

That afternoon the whole course was paraded in a hollow square. Trucks were reversed onto the parade ground with steaming hot containers of stew on board. We were told that if anybody wanted to 'jack in', all they had to do was fall out, get their kit and climb on the truck. To my utter amazement, two of my C Squadron colleagues, the ex-Royal Marine and the ex-Australian SAS, fell out. I asked them why they wanted to leave and they replied that they didn't want to work with Africans. I found this amazing, since working with Africans was what Scouts was all about. It just shows what lack of food, sleep deprivation and exhaustion can do. By this point, I believe that the instructors had made up their minds regarding which personnel they wanted to keep on the course. Our numbers were reduced by more than half that day.

Training continued in a similar vein with lots of runs, rope courses, PT and instruction in making rope, or *tambu*, from tree bark. Our group had to make a rope from bark and tow a Land Rover ten kilometres with an instructor sitting in the vehicle. We were not allowed to touch the Land Rover; it had to be pulled only by the bark rope. Naturally, the instructor amused himself by applying the brakes every so often, but it was a jolly day indeed and fun for all.

During Week 1 food was supplied to us twice after the bread and milk. One evening we had a meal of baboon stew and *sadza*, a stiff porridge made from maize meal. After only one mug, I found I could not eat any more, because my stomach had shrunk. However, I put aside two mess tins filled with *sadza*, which kept me going for three days after that, eating a little each day until, eventually, it became so hard and yellow that I had to finish it off. Luckily, there was no shortage of water to wash it down with. I guess it must be high in carbohydrate because even though it was tough and yellowed, it kept me going for several days. I enjoy *sadza* to this day; it has the consistency of mashed potato but is an acquired taste.

During Week 2 we underwent tracking training and spent days as follow-up troops for a tracking course that was under instruction. Whites on the selection course were put in charge of the follow-up platoon; we enjoyed the minor tactics, walking long distances each day in the heat and dust and controlling the African sections as platoon commanders. I relished deploying the AS men in infantry sections and controlling the platoon in attacks on the imaginary enemy. It was arduous but fun.

We were in a generally arid area and had to dig in dry riverbeds for water. We learned how to make fire by rubbing sticks together, which was hard on the hands. The best fire-sticks came from the *mboro* tree which has a light, dry, grey-coloured soft wood. The sticks are rubbed together to produce friction and after a time will glow red hot. I would then take out of my pocket some dry elephant dung which is good tinder and make a fire by blowing on the fire-sticks and igniting the tinder.

We did a lot of night marches, divided into groups of ten black troops and one white. A map and compass would be placed on the ground and an instructor would shout a map reference. The instructors would watch to see who would pick up the map and work out the route. Often there would be a small amount of food at the RV as an incentive, so I made sure I got to the map and compass first and kicked arse on the march to get there quickly.

Also in the second week, a parade was held and several names were called out. These men had to get on a truck and were RTU'd to Salisbury. Charlie Krause called out my name one day before pulling me off the truck. It was just Charlie having a little joke; he had a developed sense of humour. We were now down to around fifty men in total.

Week 3 was pretty much the same, with plenty of PT, ropes courses, marches, singing, sleep deprivation, very little food, and we were always hot, dry and dirty. Again, food was issued every few days in very small quantities.

Then came Operation Egg. One day we all had to parade at last light with our fire-sticks, our rifle, one magazine, one full water bottle and a mug. As a group we had to wade into the lake with rifles and fire-sticks above our heads so that all our kit got soaking wet but not the rifle or fire-sticks. The idea of this was to wet any hidden matches. I had my gas lighters in my boots. Then we got on trucks and were dropped off individually in the bush with one raw egg each. We were told that we would be met by the truck at first light where we were to produce a cooked egg. After being dropped off, I quickly got a huge bonfire going with my cigarette lighter. I hard boiled my egg and had a warm sleep. I heard several rounds being fired off during the night. I found out later that a few of the black soldiers were shooting at shadows. At dawn, many of black soldiers had to eat raw eggs and account for expended ammunition, with several of them RTU'd. People were still 'jacking in' every day and by the end of the week we were down to four whites and forty blacks.

Week 4 began with more practical map-reading training, which meant long day and night marches. We were paraded as one group and each of us was issued with forty pounds of blue painted rocks and half a loaf of bread. We were briefed for a two-day march to Makuti, a police post on the edge of the Zambezi escarpment, some thirty kilometres away in a direct line. However, we had to march along the line of water holes which effectively doubled the distance. On the way we saw much wildlife, including a family group of three rhinos, which, because they are short-sighted, could smell us but not see us. The male was jumping up and down angrily and I could literally feel the ground quake. We all carefully took large steps backwards through the bush until we were a safe distance away. Later a large herd of wild pigs stampeded past us, probably due to the presence of lion in the area. Clambering up out of the daunting Zambezi escarpment, we finally arrived at Makuti, hot, exhausted and drained. Apparently, some of the black soldiers had left a trail of blue rocks along the line of march. We were paraded and briefed for a return to Kariba on foot the following morning. We were not issued any rations. Nobody 'jacked in' at this point although morale was not at its highest. Then, surprisingly, we were each given half a ration pack and our spirits soared.

At dawn the next day, we set off for our first RV on the top of one of the highest mountains in the area. There was no water on the route and we suffered badly from thirst. During one rest stop one of the white soldiers happened to sit under a buffalo bean bush. The miniscule hairs on the buffalo bean pod are the most effective itching powder imaginable and somehow the soldier managed to get some of the diabolical hairs down his neck, which began to itch immediately. It drove him quite mad. One remedy is to wash the hairs off but this requires a lot of water, or mud, which we did not have. The only other thing we could do was to strip bark off a nearby tree and rub damp bark on him. We all set to work and gathered a pile of bark together and rubbed his back. This brought a small amount of relief but it took time. When he eventually regained a measure of composure, we got back on the trail.

On arriving at Kariba the next day, we, the survivors—four white and thirty-five black soldiers—were told we had passed and would form the nucleus of a new Pseudo Troop. The other three ES who passed were Rich Cullum (SAS), Terry O'Leary (RLI) and Jean Desbles (SAS). All of us had previous territorial or regular service. My lasting impression of Selous Scouts selection is one of extreme weariness, dust, dirt engrained in my hands and feet, a hollow, wasted feeling inside and grey dust, grey trees and grey rocks. Bush sores had erupted on my legs and I was generally run down and dehydrated. Strangely, I felt very alert when we reached Kariba, although this may have been due to hallucination from severe dehydration. I must say that the Scouts ran the severest selection course I have either done or heard about. It had a high wastage rate.

The South African answer

I did not have to do the South African Reconnaissance Commando selection course, as I had served in the Rhodesian SAS and Selous Scouts but I did do three days of psychological and physical testing at the Pretoria Military Medical Institute. The Recces initially had a very high wastage rate on their selection courses. They tried training the volunteers to reduce this but to no avail. They then tried to quantify the mental and physical make-up of a successful selection course participant by bringing in psychologists and doctors. I went through three days of testing which included a full day with a psychologist, an IQ test that lasted hours, physical testing on treadmills and at rest and finally, a very thorough eyesight test. The 'trick cyclist' was very interested in my military experience and seemed amused by my answers to the Rorschach test (the 'ink-blots'). He told me I was highly intelligent, with an IQ of 131, and that I liked killing. He was both right and wrong. I shall leave you, the reader, to decide which one was right and which one was wrong. I passed everything except the eyesight test. The woman who tested me asked me how I had come to Pretoria and I replied that I had driven from Salisbury. She seemed horrified that someone like me was loose on the roads without spectacles. In no uncertain terms she told me that my poor eyesight disqualified me from joining the Recces. However, I was offered the job despite her misgivings. I understand that the application of these mental and physical tests did little to change the wastage rates.

The Selous Scouts, I believe, had the right idea. Five days is not long enough to sort out the people you want and the ones you don't want. It takes at least a month. Psychological and medical tests do not help either. I was amazed when my two colleagues from C Squadron—the former Royal Marine and the former Australian SAS man—'jacked in' after only three days of sleep deprivation, no food and physical exhaustion. For me, that was a lesson learned. You just don't know what your buddies are like until you are deep in the shit. A selection course does not achieve the required aim unless it is tailored to suit the precise needs of the unit that runs it and the needs of the conflict that it is involved in. As warfare changes and conflicts change then selection courses need to change. Perhaps the current courses designed to test physical fitness and the ability of a soldier to be a 'pack animal' need to be revised. It may be that in the future language and urban survival skills will need to be incorporated. However, John Davies might well have been right in that the only way to really know somebody is to work alongside him and test him 'on the job'.

2
Rhodesian SAS

This chapter continues from the point where I woke up one Monday morning and realized I had opened my mouth about joining the SAS and had to either 'put up or shut up'. It would be wrong to represent the Rhodesian SAS as if it had no problems and everything was wonderful, so I shall tell the tale as I, and others, saw it … warts and all.

When I decided to join C Squadron (Rhodesian) SAS, I presented myself at the barracks at Cranborne outside Salisbury where I was interviewed by the Squadron 2 i/c. I showed him my certificate of discharge from 21 SAS and he told me I could join the Rhodesian army and attempt the next SAS selection course in a couple of weeks' time, before advising, "Just a few weeks' retraining and you'll go straight into the troops."

The Rhodesian SAS was a small unit at that time with only two troops, A and B, so I thought that in just a few weeks I would be joining one of them. This seemed fine to me so I popped into town to the recruiting office and filled in all the forms. Within a few days I had attested and I made my way to the barracks to show my face. I counted thirty-two operators and five officers on parade when I arrived. I was given a bed space in one of the barrack rooms, drew some kit, and was told I had the next two weeks to train myself and prepare for the selection course. There were several other foreign recruits in the same barrack room. We trained together, had a few drinks together and got to know each other before the selection course. The other men on the course all had previous military service in the British and Australian armies, including active service in Northern Ireland and Vietnam, and had received the same assurance that I had regarding "just a few weeks' retraining and you'll go straight into the troops".

In the UK there was a tradition that the men who had passed the last selection course briefed those who were training for the next one. The same thing happened in Rhodesia. Jake Harper-Ronald and Ian Suttill, recently of 1 Para and the Royal Marines respectively, filled us newcomers in on the gory details of the course, what kit to take and what were the best routes to use. The course is described in the previous chapter, so I won't revisit it, but, as mentioned, at the end of the walking phase in the Inyanga mountains we got off the truck at Cranborne barracks and the other foreign volunteers and I were given some news by a Training Troop sergeant. He informed us that we would all have to do a full recruits' course and then a complete continuation course before being admitted to the troops. We were stunned; we felt we had been 'shafted'. I went straight to the 2 i/c's office and explained that I, and the others, had enlisted on the basis of going "straight into the troops after a few weeks' retraining". His response was, "You're in now and there's nothing you can do about it." He lied. He knew he was lying and we knew he was lying.

I had three choices: I could do the recruits' course, or I could desert or I could transfer to the Rhodesian Light Infantry. I chose the recruits' course. I was determined to win my SAS beret … and then leave. I felt bitter.

The recruits' course was a tedious drudge, and what was worse, it was run mainly by a sergeant who was a bully. He was a very thorough soldier, but still a bully. He would pick on a man and ride him until the victim either deserted or threw a punch and earned himself thirty days in detention barracks, known as 'the box'. Paul Kruger was the other instructor on the course and was a thoroughly good man, and a far better leader than his colleague would ever be.

We foreigners did the recruits course with a number of Rhodesian national servicemen, initially about sixty of them, all teenagers. Our sergeant did a comprehensive job screwing them over and destroying their morale, so much so that by the end the course, over half had quit voluntarily to go to the Rhodesian Light Infantry. Others were found to be unsuitable as SAS material and were 'binned'. Many made the conscious decision to leave rather than endure the sergeant any longer. There was a glaring lack of management control over this man.

On completion of the recruits course, the national servicemen who remained did a selection course with volunteers from other units, including the Rhodesian Light Infantry. The survivors of this selection, along with me and the other foreigners, who had previously completed our selection, were then dispatched to the Parachute Training School (PTS) at New Sarum air force base just outside Salisbury for our basic static line parachute course. This was a breeze and we all thoroughly enjoyed it.

Strangely, several volunteers from the Rhodesian Light Infantry who had passed selection left voluntarily halfway through the basic parachute course. Some months later, a corporal, Bob 'Shoulders, Smith, an ex-2 Para who had seen service in Northern Ireland, said he had had enough of the SAS and chose

Preparing for a parachute deployment. *Photo* Jake Harper-Ronald

to return to the RLI where, he said, there was less bullshit. He was right.

After the basic parachute course, it was on to the continuation course where we lost more people. Continuation training was scheduled to take ten weeks but due to the increasing pace of the war, it was shortened. Training consisted of communications, medical, demolitions small arms and heavy weapons, patrolling, tracking and anti-tracking.

Communications, or 'signalling', involved learning Morse code, use of the TR48 high-frequency (HF) radio, encryption and decryption of messages, voice procedure and use of the very high-frequency (VHF) radios. For me, it was a breeze since I had been a signaller in 21 SAS. Good communications is the lifeblood of Special Forces operations: give a man a radio and you double his effectiveness. It was a joy to use the Racal radios designed in South Africa after the appalling radios used by the SAS in UK. Until 1970 the British SAS, both regular and territorial, and diplomatic personnel, used the high-frequency 123 set for transmitting long-range messages in Morse code. It was designed in 1943 and put into production in the early 1950s. It contained valves that glowed in the dark and had to be dried out over a cooker when it rained. Frequencies were changed using tiny plug-in crystals. This was a bugger when one's fingers were cold. The Rhodesian equivalent was the TR48 which was all solid-state, had frequency changing by dialling and was much more user-friendly than the 123 set. The standard VHF voice radio used by the British army at that time was a large, heavy, cumbersome thing called the A41, with a poor transmitting range. By comparison the Rhodesian army used a small lightweight radio that had a very good range. And we had one each! What joy!

The signals training system the Rhodesians used was not as professional as the one used by 21 SAS, who had a dedicated room with ten sound-proofed booths and ten tape recorders using ten forty-five-minute lessons of increasing difficulty, with tests. This system could take a student with no Morse code knowledge to ten words per minute at the best speed of the individual student. This system of programmed learning was set up by 2 bank employees who used similar techniques to train their banks' employees.

By comparison, the Rhodesians used a classroom with a large number of students and one instructor with a Morse code buzzer, the disadvantage being that progress was measured by the speed of the slowest student.

Medical training was mostly carried out at the unit, with practical experience at the hospital in Harare township over a weekend. Students would learn twenty drugs, stitching wounds, cut-downs to veins to insert drips when veins had collapsed, the draining of lungs and the treatment of gunshot trauma. Those who qualified became troop medics and would carry a troop medic kit in the SAS patrol. By comparison, the medic kit used in 21 SAS was far more basic and, although the medic might not do much harm, he might not do a lot of good either. Troop medics could later go on a three-month MA3 medical assistant's course, a high-pressure course much sought after by the troopies.

The demolitions course was a lot of fun and involved blowing up railway lines, old buildings and suchlike, using military plastic explosive and commercial explosives.

The small-arms and heavy weapons phase introduced the students to the range of weapons in use by terrorist forces: the SKS automatic rifle, the AK-47 assault rifle, the RPD belt-fed machine gun and the DShK 12.7mm heavy machine gun. Depending on ammunition availability the RPG-2 and RPG-7 rocket launchers were also used.

Patrolling training included working in a four-man patrol, crossing obstacles and learning to work together as a team. Tracking and anti-tracking were skills I had never come across before. Tracking involves following 'spoor', which is anything at ground level and 'sign' which is anything above ground level. Anti-tracking is about learning to cover one's sign and spoor to deter people who are tracking you.

On completion of continuation training, one was posted to a troop, either A or B Troop, and then into a 'call sign' or 'stick', a four-man patrol, before being badged SAS. Sadly, there was not a lot of 'warry' action going on at this time: it was the lull before the storm when ZANLA was to flood the country with insurgents in early 1976.

Two foreigners, Tony Berry and Bobby Thacker, both English but with Australian army experience in Vietnam, had been meeting with an Australian, Blue Kelly, from the RLI. Blue was in touch with a chap in England by the name of Tony Banks. Banks was recruiting white mercenaries for work in Africa and the Middle East. Because they were bored, the three of them left for England where they met Banks who then signed them up. Blue and Bobby went to Lebanon where the civil war was in progress to work for the Christian Phalangist militia. I later received a letter from the Australian in which he described how Bobby had been killed during an attack on a camp. Bobby was killed by a Browning .50 calibre round as he ascended an exterior staircase. The body could not be brought down until nightfall due to the incoming fire. He had found the war he was looking for.

At the end of continuation training, our bullying sergeant did not even bother to organize the celebration which is customary after the end of any course, so I arranged the affair myself by getting everyone to chip in with Rh$10 into a kitty. We had a very nice evening at the Pink Panther Steakhouse in Salisbury where we were joined by Ian Douglas and Paul Hogan from the PTS.

After continuation training, where I specialized in communications, I was posted to A Troop which was all regular and was made up mainly of foreigners. B Troop was all Rhodesian and comprised mainly national servicemen and territorials who were serving their six-week military stints known as call-ups.

At this time, numbers of foreign soldiers were deserting from the SAS. On Saturday mornings after breakfast we foreigners would watch the 'freedom bird' gaining altitude over the city after taking off from Salisbury airport en route to Europe and we would guess which of our friends was on it. Once it was known who had deserted, the relevant locker would be broken into and whatever was left behind would be 'liberated'. One national serviceman, the son of a world-famous novelist, deserted and left every bit of his kit behind, including his pistol. Unfortunately, one of my colleagues got there first.

Someone in the SAS hierarchy must have realized that there was something amiss: in no other SAS unit in the world did soldiers desert or revert to their infantry battalions in such numbers. One morning the 2 i/c had all foreigners on parade and threatened to take our passports away if the desertions continued. This is like continuing the flogging until morale improves. He had absolutely no idea why people were leaving. Ian Suttill laughed out loud. Later we all had a good laugh about this gem of incompetence. The desertions continued.

About this time Barry Wilbur, a Brit and former Parachute Regiment soldier, also deserted because he was fed up with being messed around and the lack of interesting work. He too became employed through Banks, this time in Angola. I later got a letter from Barry telling how he had hurt his back when he had fallen off the back of a pick-up truck which was fitted with an anti-tank weapon. He was admitted to a hospital in Kinshasa and I lost touch with him.

Because I worked in the bush with people I could relate to, I stayed in C Sqn SAS, got some experience and waited for the unit to change. My experience in civilian life told me that companies change every few years when managers either leave or are shifted around and I guessed that the Rhodesian SAS would be no different. On operations in the bush I worked mainly with Ian Suttill, Dave O'Mulligan, and Bob Pike, on generally long, hard flogs, cutting for spoor or undertaking attacks on small terrorist base camps.

Cutting for spoor entails 'cross-graining': walking in a straight line across an area to bisect spoor, tracks or marks at ground level or sign marks above ground level. The patrol usually walks in an extended line, if the ground permits, and each man searches for indications of human activity. It is boring, tiring and rarely yields any concrete results.

The work C Squadron was allocated over the years 1974–76 was, to my eyes, not strictly speaking 'SAS style' operations; essentially 'patrol company' activity. However, I enjoyed the helicopter assaults. Watching tracer fire come up from the ground has a hypnotic effect: everything appears to go into slow motion as the tracer bullet makes an arc that appears to come closer and closer to the aircraft.

I also enjoyed my first personal kill. I have never taken drugs, not even tobacco, but I got a high from that kill which I do not think could ever be equalled by any drug. It happened during an attack on a small camp in a heavily forested part of Mozambique. I was in the sweep line, driving the bad guys towards the stop groups, when one of the enemy popped up from underneath a fallen tree. I got a shock. I am not sure which of us was more startled. My British training had taught me to always keep the safety catch on my rifle

Camp attack. *Private collection*

Camp attack. *Private collection*

applied. After fumbling for what seemed several minutes, but was more like half a nano-second, I emptied half a magazine into the man. Following that experience, I always kept the safety catch off when the shooting started. That way the weapon goes 'bang' when you need it.

On one operation, the entire squadron of about fifty men, led by a new subaltern, who later became the unit's 2 i/c, crossed the border fence in the northeast of Rhodesia and headed towards the Mozambican town of Chioco to attack a small terrorist camp. It took us four days to get there and four to get back. Halfway there we crossed the Rio Luia, known as the Ruia River in Rhodesia, which was in full spate. We made 'Bergen rafts' by wrapping two rucksacks in a groundsheet and swimming the river. There was no water en route except from the Luia. We were all very weary when we arrived at the target and even more tired when we got back having swum the Luia a second time. The bush in the Zambezi valley is dry at that time. We crossed the grain of the country, going up hills and then down the other side. Small midges, known as mopane flies, were in abundance and would get into every orifice unless one had a face veil. Tsetse flies were plentiful and made a sting like a cigarette burn. That walk was unpleasant but a challenge. We would have used helicopters to get to Chioco, but only one was available and that was reserved for casualty evacuation.

1976 Elim Mission base camp, 1976, after the long walk back from Chioco. The author (left) and Jake Harper-Ronald.

Another operation stands out in my memory. In January 1976 we were ordered to attack a terrorist camp known as Mavue in southern Mozambique, on the confluence of the Lundi and Sabi rivers just across the southeastern Rhodesian border. The camp was situated around a single-storey tin-roofed building that had once been a trading post. There were a number of rondavels, or mud and grass huts, in the area.

A and B Troops, about forty men in total, set off by truck towards the target area and set up a firm base camp close to the Mozambican border, where we were briefed by the Officer Commanding who would lead the assault. We were to make a night approach march on the terrorist camp and execute a dawn attack. We would be supported by 81mm mortars from the School of Infantry and one Vampire jet aircraft from the air force. Stop groups would be positioned and a sweep line would be in place at first light. The attack would be initiated by a Vampire strike and the sweep line would then assault the camp. The stop groups would block escape routes on 2 sides and the 81mm mortars would put down fire between the camp and the River Sabi and effectively deny that escape route. Intelligence, we were told, indicated that there were thirty terrorists in the camp ready to infiltrate into Rhodesia. We were not told where this intelligence originated.

Mavue Camp, 1976. From left: Jake Harper-Ronald, Bob Pike and the author.

Mavue Camp, 1976. Clearing out the ZANLA camp.

Mavue Camp, 1976. A view from a building.

We marched through the night around three sides of a square and arrived at the target area just before first light. We heard truck noises in the distance coming from the direction of the camp. The stop groups and sweep line were in position as dawn broke. I remember hearing a strange sound like heavy leaves falling around me, and there was a very loud *whoosh*, followed by the sound of heavy weapons firing overhead. Suddenly a mushroom cloud appeared several hundred metres to our front, followed by a huge bang. Cylindrical objects went flying through the air and detonated in the air and around us. A Vampire jet had flown over us and hit the truck we had heard just before dawn. The sound of the 'heavy leaves' was the Vampire's empty 20mm cases falling around us.

There was shooting coming from the area of the camp as the sweep line closed in on the building and the huts. The mortars laid down some fire which was by no means the rapid fire we were expecting. I was in Stop Group 6 with Jake Harper-Ronald, Bob Pike and a Rhodesian. We fired a few desultory rounds at some movement to our front but the bush around us was too thick to see clearly. Jake had been in 1 Para in Northern Ireland where he was in the intelligence section and often carried a camera there. He had one with him at Mavue and some of his pictures are in this book.

Following the assault we closed in on the building and huts where 'looting' or clearing the area was in progress by all ranks. We got into all-round defence and waited for the order to exfiltrate. An Alouette III helicopter arrived to take out the heavy weapons, documents and our two casualties. One casualty was due to severe dehydration and the other was one of our young men who had been shot in the leg. We were credited with twenty-two kills. Later that year when I signed up with the Selous Scouts, the Political Commissar (PC) in the pseudo troop that I joined had been present in the camp, sitting under the prominent tree in the middle of the clearing when the Vampire strike went in. He, like most of the rest of the terrorists, headed straight for the Sabi River, despite the best efforts of the School of Infantry mortar teams and he swam downstream. So much for denying the escape route through mortar fire. The PC told me later we killed forty-five terrorists and not twenty-two as we had originally thought.

The reconnaissance for this camp attack had been carried out, not by the SAS but by two Selous Scouts, one white and one black. I met that particular *murungu*, or white man, when I joined the Selous Scouts and we compared notes. He had initially estimated the number of terrorists in the camp to have been between twenty and thirty.

Following our exfiltration, we marched to our firm base where we all had a good night's sleep before returning to 'Bright Lights' and our barracks in Salisbury. The return trip involved pushing the trucks out of countless sandy riverbeds. On one overnight stop, as was usual, the men detailed for 'stag', or sentry duty, slept in a line, making it easy for one guard to waken the next

Mavue Camp, 1976. An ammo truck goes up after Vampire strike.

Return from Mavue, 1976. Pushing trucks out of the sand again.

guard. All guards had to be out of their sleeping bags and perform guard duty in full webbing. When my hour of guard duty ended I woke up the next soldier, an Aussie citizen from Papua New Guinea, and I slid into my sleeping bag. Sometime later I heard a flurry of movement and much slapping but I thought nothing of it and did not wake up. In the morning I saw a group of soldiers peering into the Aussie's ammo pouch, where inside was a baboon spider as big as a fist with hairy legs and large staring eyes. These creatures have potent venom capable of killing the very young and the old. While Aussie was doing his guard duty the spider had crawled into the warmth of his sleeping bag. When Aussie got back into his bag he felt something and the commotion that ensued was him getting the spider off his chest, which then scuttled into his ammo pouch. Aussie deserted later. The spider was kept as a pet by a former Royal Marines sniper, Clive Mason, who had also served in the Australian SAS and had done a tour in Vietnam. Clive carried a Lee-Enfield sniper rifle in preference to an FN. On one camp attack I saw him operate his bolt-action Lee-Enfield rifle so quickly that he was firing 'double taps' or fast consecutive rounds almost as fast as I could fire from my semi-automatic FN rifle. He was certainly skilled on a bolt-action rifle. He was killed a year later on a camp attack, when he was shot in the head: the sniper himself had been 'sniped' ...

Another operation, in August 1976, involved a deployment to the eastern districts just south of the border town of Umtali where we were based in a caravan park. We were told that we were 'on standby' but no further information was forthcoming. One evening we were listening to the radio and heard that the Selous Scouts had hit a big terrorist camp in Mozambique called Nyadzonya, and had claimed 350 kills. This was an unheard-of number at that stage in the war. It was plain that the Scouts were getting all the good work and we were the 'standby' element. Not only that but the Scouts had recce'd the camp at Mavue and had done a thoroughly professional job. Later it transpired that Army HQ had offered the Nyadzonya raid to the SAS but our OC had turned it down as being too risky. Ron Reid-Daly, the Selous Scouts OC, had leapt at the opportunity. It was certainly risky but he who dared won the day.

Immediately after the Scouts had hit the Nyadzonya base, where they killed in excess of 1,000, not the 350 originally claimed, Frelimo rocketed and mortared the town of Umtali. We were ordered into Umtali to raise civilian morale, so early one morning we left our caravan park and roared down the mountain road into Umtali. Civilians lined the streets in their night attire and waved and cheered us during our triumphal entry that resembled the liberation of Paris in the Second World War. Unfortunately, we all got scattered as nobody had told us where to assemble. But it was good while it lasted.

As mentioned, in my opinion the work that the SAS was getting at that stage of the war in 1976 was not true SAS work. We were more like the Parachute Regiment Patrol Company. I craved more action, more excitement and it was time to move on. The grass would be greener on the other side and I suspected the Selous Scouts was the place to be, so I applied to do the Selous Scouts selection course in September.

After I had been in the Selous Scouts for two years, the management team at the SAS changed completely. Gone was the old management and in came a new team like a breath of fresh air.

I returned to the SAS in 1978, sensing I could get more of what I wanted, such as parachuting, reconnaissance, demolitions, interdictions and the like. On my return, I detected a complete change in atmosphere with the new regime in charge. Some of the deadwood senior NCOs were still there but the unit was getting a better quality of work; and the desertion rate was right down.

The SAS had been expanded on paper from one squadron comprising A & B Troops to a notional regimental strength of three squadrons: A, B and C. This so-called expansion had been carried out so that a full regimental

C Squadron 1 Rhodesian SAS, Kabrit barracks, Salisbury, Rhodesia, March 1980.

allocation of equipment could be provided. For once the unit had sufficient vehicles, fuel, ammunition, radios and more. However, each squadron was in reality an under strength troop and the SAS never deployed more than a hundred men in the field. This figure was only ever achieved by calling up all the ex-national servicemen on territorial duties and every man that was on leave. I was posted to the new C Squadron. At last, the SAS was now getting the operations I thrived on: specialized jobs designed to remove individuals and resources important to the enemy and to carry out reconnaissance missions and interdictions. Late 1978, 1979 and early 1980 were good times and were the best of times, as described later in this account.

3
Selous Scouts Pseudo Operations

After passing the Selous Scouts selection course in September 1976, I was posted to Recce Troop for a short period before going on operations under Major 'S', out of Chiredzi fort in the southeast of the country in the Operation Repulse area. Then, in early 1977, I joined a pseudo troop, also operating in the southeast: 6 Troop was commanded by a Warrant Officer Second Class (WO2) with a Colour Sergeant (C/Sergeant) as the 2 i/c. The troop comprised about forty African soldiers at full strength, some of whom were enlisted men and some turned terrorists (TTs). It was a mixed Shona and Ndebele troop at that time. The troop had an AS sergeant, four AS corporals, several lance-corporals and the rest privates. One of the TTs, a former ZANLA political commissar, actually handled the position of Political Comissar (PC) in the troop. All TTs were given nominal army ranks and were paid by Special Branch. Their families lived at Inkomo barracks which, apart from the security aspect, was an incentive for them not to return to ZANLA. They were an incredibly happy bunch who enjoyed their jobs and were generally a pleasure to be with.

As I joined the unit, the WO2 went off on assignment with Special Branch (SB) and the Colour Sergeant took over command. My first sight of the troop was one morning in Main Camp at Nkomo barracks, near Salisbury, when I saw the black soldiers coming out of their barrack room. All were in civilian dress, armed with AK-47 rifles, RPD machine guns, RPG-7 rocket launchers, Chinese stick grenades in pockets, webbing over their civilian clothes and blankets wrapped around them. One multi-skilled individual had all this kit and rifle strung about him plus a battery-operated record player on his head with a record playing!

We all clambered onto trucks and headed off to the Selous Scout fort at Chiredzi. The 450-kilometre journey took eight hours, due to punctures caused mainly from overloading and the cheap remould tyres!

The Chiredzi fort was a typical Scouts fort. It looked like a contractor's yard, with high walls, double gates and rooms around a central courtyard, which housed the operations room with maps and radios, the radio operator's shack with tele-printer and radios, the Special Branch (SB) office, prison cells, the AS and ES barrack rooms, a medical room with several beds for sick personnel, ablutions and the cookhouse. It was a self-contained installation with space enough in the central courtyard for a helicopter to land.

The permanent staff included the fort commander, Major S, an air force liaison officer, Squadron Leader Fenton-Wells, a quartermaster NCO, cooks, radio operators and SB staff both black and white. Three troops, 4, 5 and 6, rotated through this fort before deployments and after completing bush trips.

The Chiredzi airport, Buffalo Range, was the main airstrip for the Op Repulse area and could handle Canberra jet bombers and Hawker Hunter jet fighters. There was a substantial air force camp on the airfield as well as an army Fire Force camp for airborne assault troops which fluctuated in size as operations demanded.

After two days at the fort, we were briefed and deployed by truck to an area close to the Nyadjena Tribal Trust Land (TTL) near Fort Victoria. We then rendezvoused with a helicopter which flew us into Nyadjena. We walked all night and climbed a high feature, posing as a ZANLA terrorist resupply group freshly arrived from Mozambique. The ES remained on the hill with four black soldiers as guard while the rest of the troop made an approach on a kraal in the valley below.

Things went wrong from the start. The locals ran off as soon they were approached. It became obvious that the Nyadjena TTL was more or less a ZANLA 'liberated zone'. In the first two days we had a contact with a local resident ZANLA group and took a couple of lightly wounded casualties, mainly from mortar rounds. One local was captured. He protested that if he was to die it would be for Zimbabwe. He was taken by us for interrogation by SB. These people were politically motivated and it was quite clear the locals were supporting the terrorists. ZANLA, the Zimbabwe African National Liberation Army, was the military wing of Robert Mugabe's ZANU, the Zimbabwe African National Union. ZANLA, operating out of Mozambique and Tanzania, was Chinese communist-trained and supplied and operated on classic Maoist lines, infiltrating the rural masses and indoctrinating the *povo*, the people, through terror, subversion and propaganda, perpetrated through highly skilled and motivated Political Commissars. ZANLA operated initially in the east, southeast, northeast and north of the country, while their Soviet-backed liberation competitors, Joshua Nkomo's ZAPU (Zimbabwe African People's Union) operated from Zambia into the west, northwest and southwest of Rhodesia.

The Rhodesian security forces were overstretched at the best of times; the Nyadjena TTL had been left without a security force presence—police, army or Internal Affairs—for too long and the resident terrorist groups had made the Nyadjena their own

After two weeks in the Nyadjena and achieving nothing, 6 Troop was redeployed to an area some thirty kilometres away where we operated in a similar manner. Some successful approaches were made on various villages and we were able to call in the Fire Force, an airborne helicopter and parachute assault force, several times achieving some kills and captures.

Every Fire Force operation usually achieved something. A small Fire Force might comprise one Alouette III helicopter with a 20mm cannon (the K-Car) and three or four Alouette IIIs with troops on board (G-Cars), each with a 'stick' of four soldiers. A large Fire Force might comprise one K-Car and half a dozen G-Cars, with a Dakota DC-3 with 20 paratroopers and possibly Hawker Hunter ground-attack jets and Canberra jet bombers. The Fire Force was commanded by an army officer in the K-Car who controlled troop movements on the ground and coordinated the air strikes.

Our AS preferred the SAS as their Fire Force of choice. They told me that if the SAS were the Fire Force, then the shooting was usually a few double taps (two aimed rounds fired in quick succession) for around five minutes and there were ten kills out of ten terrorists. If the Fire Force was found from the Rhodesian Light Infantry (RLI), then the shooting was in bursts, lasted an hour and they killed five out of ten. If the Rhodesian African Rifles (RAR) were called in, then the shooting went on all day and they killed one out of ten.

We once deployed into a TTL by train at night, though we generally deployed by truck and sometimes by bus. I believe in the north of the country a beer truck was used for deployments. We had an armoured bus on one operation. The bus had been found in Mozambique by a Scouts armoured column in October 1976 and was taken to Inkomo barracks where it was fitted with armour plate. We used it to deploy from Inkomo to Chiredzi and for deployments out of the Scouts fort. On one operation all the wiring burnt out when the dip switch was operated. We returned to our camp by the light of a pocket torch, very slowly. Another day the bus was moving fast down a hill when the steering wheel came off. The driver turned around and showed me the wheel! Luckily, the bus left the road at what was the only safe point available and came to a stop in the bush, having missed all the rocks, trees and anthills. On another day I was sitting behind the driver when the bus went over a very large bump. The RPD machine gun owned by an AS sitting directly behind me, loosed off a short burst. The rounds passed through my barrack box upon which I was sitting, bounced off the armour plate against which I was leaning and exited the bus through the windscreen in front of the driver. It appears the trigger sear on the machine gun was worn.

Terrorist incursions usually took place in groups of between ten and twenty. The largest incursion I heard of was a group of 150 to the north of our location. They were spotted by a Selous Scouts troop and I listened to the Fire Force call-out on the VHF radio. I remember the Fire Force comprised one K-Car, three G-cars and one ParaDak and was outnumbered by five to one, but those were normal odds. They got twenty or so kills for the loss of one soldier dead. The 'gooks', or terrorists, had 'bomb-shelled' in the thick bush which made the operation difficult. 'Bomb-shelling' was a standard terrorist tactic: the enemy would scatter in pairs or individually, to meet up at a pre-arranged RV after the security forces had departed the contact area.

From time to time we changed from pseudo to observation post (OP) role, and sometimes a combination of both. Our troop always posed as a terrorist group and, as mentioned, we had a political commissar who had been trained by the Chinese in East Africa. This was the self-same ZANLA PC who had survived the SAS attack on Mavue camp in 1976. He was a very nice man to talk to and I liked him. I asked him why he had joined ZANLA and he replied that it was because ZANLA had come to his kraal, or village, on a recruiting drive. When I asked our enlisted men why they had joined the Rhodesian African Rifles, they said it was because the RAR came recruiting in their TTL. It seems they were all looking for adventure and joined the first recruiting organization that appeared on the scene.

When the troop made a capture, he was handed over to SB for interrogation at the Chiredzi fort. He would be put in a cell and handcuffed to a ring in the floor. Interrogations were often lengthy and comprised long interviews with sleep-deprivation disorientation. If a capture rated as a 'face', that is to say an important person, he would be made an immediate offer he could not refuse and he normally accepted the offer to join our band of brothers. He would then return to the troop that had captured him, with the firing pin of

ZANLA terrorists training in Mozambique. *Photos* Dennis Croukamp

his rifle removed, for redeployment. However, a 'face' was only useful for a limited time after his capture before news of his compromise spread. At the fort, Special Branch, the troop commander and the senior AS would discuss whether they wanted the capture or not.

If they wanted him he would do three probationary bush trips with his firing pin removed and with two AS detailed as his bodyguards. When the troop was on rest & recuperation (R&R) he would spend his time handcuffed in the cell. After three successful bush trips he would be put on the SB payroll with his firing pin returned. If he was unsuccessful then SB would send him to their headquarters at Bindura for 'redeployment'.

Some of our AS were reasonably well educated and I would have long talks to them about Shona culture and customs. Others spoke little or no English and were illiterate. I once did an OP for three weeks with three TTs. Two were illiterate and spoke no English and the third was a 'Jesus Freak'. I am a Christian but this man nearly drove me insane.

On one pseudo op I was the only white soldier. I was guarded by the man with the battery-powered record player on a hill near the rest of the troop who were operating below in the pseudo role. The AS enjoyed the pseudo role since they could act the 'big time' with the local girls, drink beer, have their hair plaited, listen to records and generally enjoy themselves, provided, of course, they had been well received by the locals. They had all this and pay as well! However, after a few weeks on this particular operation, the records were all broken save for *Famba Zvakanaka* (go well) by Susie and the Green Arrows. This one record was played time after time after time and refused to die. It was a typical Shona hit record, highly repetitive and it speeded up in the middle. After weeks of it, I could stand it no longer and threw the record player off the cliff. It was me or that bloody record!

On another operation the troop was in the pseudo role and the two whites, the troop commander and me, were on top of a prominent feature under cover of a few bushes, with three AS bodyguards. After a short while we heard the small radio, the VHF, talking to us. Our senior NCO on the ground, Sergeant Dennis, told us that they had made a good approach on a kraal and had been well received. The next day, he spoke to us again, saying that there were two witches in the area and that the local people wanted him and his men to prove their strength by killing these two women. The locals claimed that the witches had caused the crops to fail and the cattle to become infertile and they wanted them dead. Dennis said he needed an answer, fast. Shortly Dennis received

Two pages from a ZANLA terrorist's notebook. *Photos* Dennis Croukamp

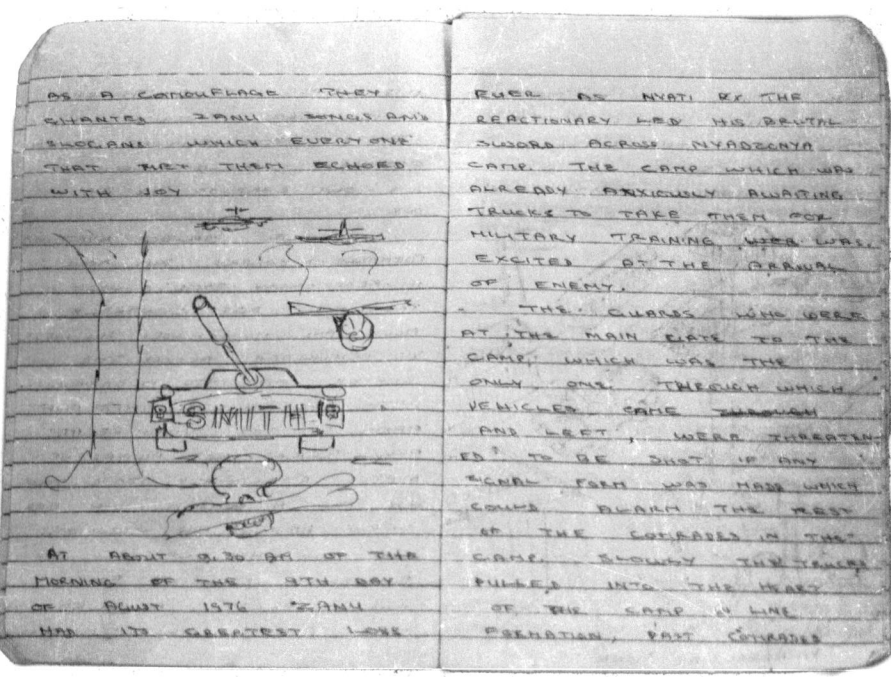

his answer. He was told to stage an 'execution' in the bush and bring the two witches onto our hill. A little while later we heard bursts of automatic fire and much cheering from below. When Dennis spoke to us again we asked him how their 'proof of strength' had been received. Dennis replied that the 'executions' had been well received and that the two individuals would be delivered to us that night.

However, all was not sunshine and roses. On one operation we had a young ES attached to us. Half the troop was operating in the pseudo role and the other half in the OP role. The troops in the OP role were watching for unusual movement in the kraals and for the movement of *mujibas*, juvenile messengers who ran with the terrorists. The pseudo men made an approach on a kraal and we awaited developments. The young ES was with his three soldiers, two TTs and one enlisted man, on a prominent hill some three kilometres from where the troop commander and I were based up. It transpired that the hill the young ES was on had also been selected by a group of terrorists as a good place to base up.

After dark the ES sent his three soldiers down the hill to fetch water while he remained at the camp on the top. As his men went down one side, the gooks came up the other. His bivouac sheet collected a good 'squirt' from the gooks but he returned fire. On hearing the shooting I got on the radio and tried to contact him. There was no reply. Twenty minutes later the three black soldiers pitched up at our hill to tell us that their ES was "probably dead". The troop commander went berserk and told them to go back and return either with the ES alive or with his body. As it happened, the ES was unharmed, having successfully returned fire to drive off the enemy, although his bivvie sheet was well and truly ventilated.

On return to Main Camp, Inkomo barracks, the troop paraded, minus the three AS, in front of Lieutenant-Colonel Ron Reid-Daly. The three AS were then marched on as the colonel stripped them of their Selous Scout belts and berets in true *Beau Geste* style, just like in the movie. This melodrama impressed on the black troops the severity of the crime. The three culprits were then transferred to Guard Force to spend their time guarding the barracks. Perhaps Reid-Daly had seen the movie.

On another operation we had the whole troop in the pseudo role and called in a 3 Commando RLI Fire Force onto a group of gooks that our troop had been

Female ZANLA terrorists training in Mozambique. *Photo* Dennis Croukamp

meeting with. Our troops became the stop groups and were positioned around the contact area as 3 Commando entered the fray by helicopter and ParaDak. Unfortunately, one of our call signs, commanded by Sergeant Dennis, took an immense amount of fire from an RLI stick when the K-Car commander lost control of the battle. Dennis was wounded, thankfully not severely. The RLI stick that shot Dennis was commanded by a chum of mine, 'Shoulders' Smith, an ex-2 Para man from UK. His machine gunner, who wounded Dennis, was Pete Donnelly, an ex-Scots Guardsman from Glasgow who sported a huge bottle scar under his jaw. The third member of the stick was 'Griffo' Griffiths from Australia who was a 'wild child' when out of the bush. The fourth member of Shoulders's stick was a young Rhodesian national serviceman. Shoulders, Pete and Griffo were hard-drinking, heavy smoking, play-hard, work-hard people that I used to drink with on R&R. Sadly, Shoulders and Pete are no longer with us, probably on eternal R&R in some dingy, smoky bar in the sky where the beer is free.

It was not unusual to hear the voices of people I knew on the radio when we called in Fire Force. Apart from the people mentioned above, I often heard André Dennison, OC A Company 2 RAR, on the radio. He was ex-Brit SAS and a keen skydiver. He was a particularly aggressive individual who handled a Fire Force well and achieved a high kill rate, although I felt he sometimes got too involved with the firefight on the ground and neglected his principal job of controlling the battle. On one occasion he was having trouble getting his black paratroopers, taking heavy fire in their sweep line, to get up and advance towards the enemy. He landed his chopper close to the sweep line and literally 'kicked arse' until they stood up and advanced. It was an amazing thing to listen to.

On another occasion he turned up at the skydiving club in Salisbury with a new square parachute which he did not know how to pack. He asked me how to pack it but I did not know either. He somehow stuffed the canopy into the container and went off and jumped it. It worked. That took some courage! Sadly, he was to die later in the war in a friendly fire incident.

Our black soldiers had trouble with sexually transmitted diseases, particularly syphilis. On one operation we had a situation where four of them had syphilis to the point where one of them could barely walk due to swollen glands in his groin. We took early R&R, had them all tested and jabbed up before returning to the bush. The AS were getting infected, cured and then re-infected by the washer women at Main Camp. These were women who had been caught 'running with terrorists' and were given jobs at the camp.

At times the troop 2 i/c, Andy Balaam, demonstrated a highly developed understanding of the African mentality. It was as if he could understand what they were doing, almost by telepathy. For instance, on one operation the AS were in pseudo role and the 2 i/c, who was the troop commander at that stage, and I were on a hill waiting for the radio to speak to us. Things were unnaturally quiet. After several days Andy suddenly called the troop back to our hill and paraded them. He ordered all the men to roll up their sleeves, empty their pockets and turn out the contents of their rucksacks. All of them had wristwatches and one man, the senior corporal, had an armful. We collected several hundred dollars in cash as well. They had been robbing buses instead of operating in the pseudo role. The senior corporal duly left our employment.

Our African soldiers were happy in the bush and I felt they could live there forever. Co-habiting and socializing with the locals, they were, in many respects living the highlife. For many it was better than living at home. However, I think a white man loses his efficiency after thirty days or so in the bush. We usually did thirty to forty days deployed before returning to Inkomo barracks for R&R.

Our black soldiers were mostly unmarried and lived in one large barrack room. The married TTs had huts in the camp and enlisted married men had good-quality apartments after 1978 when the new barracks at Inkomo were completed. The apartments were on the lines of UK council flats and were fully equipped with stoves, fridges and beds.

The enlisted AS were paid Regular Army rates of pay, with parachute pay for those so qualified and bonuses for jobs well done and for kills. The bonus system was an extremely good motivator for black and white alike. For example, if we called out Fire Force on a sighting or killed terrorists ourselves in a contact, the Special Branch paid the Scouts a Rh$50 bonus to each man for one to four dead terrorists, $100 for five to nine kills and $150 for more than ten dead. The kills were not based on a body count but on weapons collected. The application for bonus payment had to be backed up by the army daily sitrep confirming, time, location and number of kills. The TTs were also paid bonuses for kills and $40 per month. This was good pay for an African at the time, bearing in mind that a field hand earned $10 a month plus rations.

By way of a change I did a tracking follow-up with Dennis Croukamp, who was the only other Scout in the Chiredzi fort the day that a combat tracker team was required. We were deployed by chopper, started on the spoor on foot and later tracked the gooks, who were dragging a 76mm recoilless rifle with them, on motorcycles. That was certainly something different.

However, after two years I felt like a change. I was continually blackened up with camo cream and was having trouble with my skin. We walked a lot, laid up on mountains, ate poor rations and drank dirty water. Life in the Selous Scouts was, on the whole, better for a black soldier than for a white. So I returned to C Squadron SAS to get some combat parachuting, camp attacks, personal kills, ambushing and interdictions under my belt.

4
The operation that went wrong

The Rhodesian war was fought on a shoestring with a great deal of equipment either locally made or adapted to suit local needs. Equipment was used in unorthodox ways and civilian aircraft were hired when the air force could not provide. Men and equipment were continually pushed to the limit. Risks were taken and not surprisingly sometimes things went badly wrong.

After passing Selous Scouts selection, and some further training where I learned to be a terrorist—a story in itself—I was posted to Reconnaissance Troop in 1976. After a time at Recce Troop, I went to a rural hospital near the town of Bindura to gain hands-on medical experience. However, I was admitted to the hospital after only three days with malaria, which I must have contracted in early October at Kariba. On being discharged from the hospital, I was feeling very rundown. Throughout the whole of September, while on selection, I had been on near-starvation rations and this, coupled with a minimal fluid intake and hard manual work, was followed by the malaria.

My parachute logbook tells me that the day after returning from Bindura, 15 October 1976, I did a forty-second free-fall with Sergeant Dennis Croukamp and Corporal Wilson, another white Scout, at New Sarum, with AK-47 rifles, webbing and rucksacks. This was followed by another practice jump on 21 October with Croukamp, Wilson, Lieutenant S and a black Scout, at Seki Tribal Trust Land outside Salisbury. I remember we jumped as a stick of five and followed a box containing a simulated heavy load from 15,000 feet above ground level. We had oxygen in the plane, since 15,000 feet above Salisbury is 20,000 feet above sea level, and jumped from Chaminuka, a DC-3 Dakota with engines adapted for high-altitude flying. As before, we jumped with AKs, webbing and rucksacks. After the jump we returned to our base at Inkomo barracks, near Salisbury, and had our first briefing regarding the forthcoming operation.

In the SAS, both in the UK and in Rhodesia, I was used to receiving comprehensive and highly detailed briefings. However, the briefing for this, my first operation in Scouts, was minimal. Croukamp would lead the other call sign, comprising Corporal Wilson and myself. Another Scout, Jean Desbles, had injured his leg and would not be coming with us.

The area of operations covered Gaza province in southern Mozambique. Terrorists were being transported by rail from Maputo to the Rhodesian border in the vicinity of Malvernia, a small border town on the Mozambican side where they detrained and infiltrated on foot. We were to parachute in on the night of Saturday, 23 October 1976 and await pick-up by a Scouts armoured column due to enter Mozambique on Sunday, 31 October. Both call signs were tasked with cutting the railway line using explosives, cutting the telephone lines running alongside the line and observing and reporting on Frelimo and ZANLA troop movements. Some discussion took place regarding derailing the train. I tried to explain the method I had been taught overseas. However, my input was disregarded as this was apparently all in hand and the prepared charges and initiating sets were ready.

The column comprised some sixty men and twelve vehicles, mostly 2.5-ton Mercedes Unimog trucks, two locally made armoured personnel carriers, and a 15-ton Scania truck. The vehicles were fitted with either 20mm aircraft cannon or belt-fed rifle-calibre machine guns. All the men, both black and white, carried either AK-47 rifles or belt-fed RPD machine guns. Anti-tank capability was in the form of several RPG-7 rocket launchers, with two 81mm mortar tubes carried on the Scania.

We were to jump from 15,000 feet above ground level, which was approximately 18,000 feet above sea level at that point in Mozambique. The first call sign to be dropped would be Lieutenant S and his colleague, who would be deployed approximately eighty kilometres from the border, north of a town called Jorge do Limpopo and ten kilometres east of the railway. The second call sign, Croukamp, Wilson and myself, would be deployed some 100 or so kilometres from the border, south of Jorge do Limpopo, approximately ten kilometres east of the railway. No maps were available but we did have air photographs taken some weeks before by Canberra aircraft, which showed our target and our intended dropping zones. We were told to "secure the road" (with three men!) and that we would "probably" be picked up by a light aircraft if the column could not pick us up.

That was the end of our briefing. Croukamp, Wilson and I disappeared for a brew of tea and a chance to pore over the air photos. Stopping off at the medical room, we got some zinc oxide plaster to stick the photos together. They showed numerous waterholes, isolated trees and, luckily, no human habitation.

THE OPERATION THAT WENT WRONG 61

Building the first 'Pig' armoured personnel carrier, Selous Scouts MT workshop. *Photo* Dennis Croukamp

Selous Scouts 'Pig' armoured car on Mercedes Unimog chassis. *Photo* Dennis Croukamp

Two images of a Selous Scouts vehicle column on the march. *Photos* Dennis Croukamp

We drew radio equipment, which included an A76 VHF radio (very high frequency and voice only) for each man and a TR48 HF radio (high frequency and capable of voice and Morse for long-distance communication), which I carried as well as the spare batteries. Then it was a trip to the explosives store to pick up the specially prepared charges for blowing the railway line and the detonating set. We were assured that the 'Heath Robinson' detonating set would work. Apparently, all we had to do was strap this homemade wooden contraption to the inside edge of the track, remove the safety pin and the loco wheel would depress the plunger and—Bingo!—the rail would disappear and the train would roll over. It was all going to be as simple as that. I had strong reservations.

The following day I went into town to the municipal library and using an atlas I made myself an escape map, which is a simple sketch map for emergency use. Nothing in the way of escape equipment was provided by Recce Troop, which I found strange after my previous training. I had a very bad feeling about this trip.

In the army we say, "Prior Preparation and Planning Prevents Piss-Poor Performance." I did not feel happy with the preparations. There had been no 'dry run' installing the explosives and briefing information had been minimal. I therefore made up my own escape map at the local library. If the column did not get through to pick us up then the extraction alternative of "securing a road" for a light aircraft was only a 'maybe'.

On Saturday, 23 October we assembled at camp and packed our rucksacks, chest webbing and belt webbing. Typically, everyone's kit weighed around eighty pounds. My kit included five days' water, ten days' rations, an AK rifle, 500 rounds, two fragmentation grenades, two smoke grenades, a personal medical kit, groundsheet, cooker, personal radio, high-frequency radio, spare batteries, explosives and radio codes. We all jumped carrying rifle, chest webbing and belt webbing on our bodies. The rucksacks were carried behind our legs in free-fall, secured in 'Carrying Straps Personal Equipment Parachutist' (CSPEP), which is a system of straps and buckles. Moving off from camp in a civilian truck, we arrived at Rhodesian Air Force, New Sarum, late that afternoon. The air force dispatchers, Flight Lieutenant Hales and a sergeant, had made up a box for each call sign containing spare radio batteries, emergency food and tinned water. The boxes, each of which had a reserve parachute and timing device to activate the parachutes, were to be left on the drop zone as an emergency cache. Bottles of oxygen were fastened to the floor of the plane and long tubes with face masks on the end were provided for the jumpers and the dispatchers. We emplaned around 1800 hours in Chaminuka, the high-flying DC-3 Dakota, and flew southeast to Gaza province in Mozambique. The air force plan was to fly over the confluence of the Limpopo and Nuanetsi rivers in Mozambique, since these were easily identifiable features, then turn onto a heading and drop the first team, Lieutenant S and his colleague, at a predetermined time after crossing the railway line. The aircraft would then turn onto a new heading and would drop our call sign after a further elapsed time. Everything depended on dead reckoning based on time and distance. There was no Global Positioning System, or GPS, in those days.

Sadly the weather was against us and due to heavy ground haze with the rainy season approaching, the confluence of the rivers could not be identified that night. In those days, there was no technology that could give us our position accurately. The only navigation aids were the aircraft compass and the dispatchers' eyes. As soon as the dispatcher turned back from the door and shook his head, I knew the jump was aborted. We returned to Salisbury and the drop was rescheduled for the following day, Sunday, 24 October.

The next night we went through the same routine. While the aircraft was still in Rhodesia, we kitted up and waddled towards the door with the long rubber oxygen tubes paying out behind us and laden with rifles, chest webbing, belt webbing and rucksacks. Doubled over with the weight, I could see the ground far below us through a side window of the DC-3, with the Nuanetsi and Limpopo rivers like silver threads against a grey background in the moonlight. There was still some haze but the river confluence was easily seen, and Lieutenant S with his colleague followed their box out of the Dakota into the night sky. The aircraft banked onto a new heading and the three of us, Croukamp, Wilson and I, stood up and waddled up to the door.

Hales the dispatcher gave us the signal for five minutes to P hour, which is Parachute Hour or the time to jump. The dispatchers gave us "Stand in the door" as the red light came on, then "Go!" as the light changed to green. First the box was kicked out by Hales and then we followed it into the night sky. I could see my two comrades in free-fall and also the box, which was skidding around underneath us. It sometimes did this if the tiny pilot 'chute fixed to one end did not stabilize it correctly. The parachute on the box was set to open at 1,500 feet above ground level, and Croukamp followed it all the way to opening. Wilson opened lower than my opening of 2,500 feet. I could see the three other 'chutes in the sky and turned to follow the box to the ground.

THE OPERATION THAT WENT WRONG

View across Rio Savi at Masangena in Mozambique. Selous Scouts troops attack the ZANLA camp on opposite side.

A 'Pig' in Mozambique, 1976. *Photo* Dennis Croukamp

Our canopies were tactical assault parachutes made by GQ of Woking, UK. They were enormous parachutes, slightly steerable, with little in the way of forward drive, but were designed to carry a very heavy suspended load. The ground wind was around 10 mph as I drifted away from Croukamp and the box while under canopy. On landing, I collected my parachute and, after field-packing it, I hefted my rucksack on my back, the parachutes on top and moved off in the direction of Croukamp, Wilson and the box. Croukamp had contacted the DC-3 on his personal radio and told them that we were all fine. After burying our parachutes we remained at the drop zone for twenty-four hours. This gave us the opportunity not only to rest, but also to watch and listen for any reaction to our insertion. There was no reaction from FPLM, the Mozambican army, or from ZANLA or from any civilians.

The next evening we set off for the target, which we thought would be a night march of more or less ten kilometres. That part of Mozambique is as flat as a billiard table, with very soft sand underfoot and lots of clumps of bushes around ten to fifteen high. Consequently, it is impossible to walk in a straight line for more than twenty-five to fifty metres. A one-kilometre walk might end up as a two-kilometre walk, due to circumventing all the bushes and small trees. It was also difficult to walk accurately on a compass bearing; it was better to walk towards a star low on the horizon for fifteen minutes or so before changing to another star. Marching was made more difficult by the oppressive heat and the flies. We found plenty of waterholes, but they were all empty since the rains had not arrived yet.

By Wednesday morning, we were getting worried about our position, as we had not found the railway line after two nights of marching and having covered, in my estimate, forty kilometres since the drop zone. We walked the whole of Wednesday night and still did not find the railway line. Things were now getting desperate. Water was getting low, we did not know how far we were from the target and time was marching on. We did not mention any of our problems when we raised HQ at midday each day for our daily situation report. We started walking again on Thursday morning and stopped around midday to take some shelter from the heat of the sun. There was still no railway line; and I was down to my last remaining water bottle. On Thursday afternoon we started walking again. Progress was slow because we were all tired. I was starting to feel the effects of heat and fatigue, but we kept on going. We walked all Thursday night and into Friday morning. I was beginning to stagger and could not walk in a straight line. My mouth was completely dry and I could barely talk. I felt as if I needed to urinate. This was the last fluid in my body and rather than waste it I urinated into my mug and drank it. It was very dark brown, almost black, it stank and was frothy. I drank it and retched. By this time I was feeling like I was floating, classic symptoms of dehydration.

Then suddenly out of the bush we saw the railway line. It was wonderful to stop and take a rest knowing we had reached the target. Leaving our rucksacks behind an anthill, we went forward to look at the line. There were no signs of human habitation in the area and no signs of recent vehicle or foot movement on the dirt road that ran parallel to the railway. After cutting the telephone line, we moved back to our rucksacks. We assembled the explosive charges and the initiating set and while two of us placed them on the line, one kept watch. The initiating, or detonating, set looked to me like a sloppy, very loose fit inside the web of the railway line but we had been told it would work, so we left it as instructed. We went back to our rucksacks behind the anthill and waited for a train.

The next day, Friday, a train, a diesel locomotive with three carriages, arrived late in the afternoon, travelling down the line towards Maputo. It was moving too fast to ascertain whether there were any soldiers on board or not. It passed over the detonating set and continued on its way, unharmed. We later discovered that the detonating set had not worked because it was designed

The author on a railway line in Mozambique. 1976. *Photo* Dennis Croukamp

Blown rail line, 1976. *Photo* Dennis Croukamp

to fit inside a lightweight rail, not the heavy, ninety-pound rails used on Mozambican tracks. The loco wheels had pushed the whole box down without depressing the striker onto the detonator. The charges were then exploded remotely by battery, blowing large gaps in the line.

Later that same afternoon another train, or perhaps it was the same one, came up the line from the direction of Maputo. It was travelling very slowly and slowed further still as it approached the gaps in the tracks. It passed over the gaps without stopping and we could see it had three carriages, each filled with FPLM soldiers who were all leaning out of the windows, clearly on the lookout for something.

The next day, Saturday, we moved up the line northward into another laying-up position to observe movement on the road and railway line. Water was still short and there was no sign of any rain, although clouds were building up. We were not due to be picked up until Sunday, another twenty-four hours away. The same day, Saturday, 30 October, Croukamp made a decision. By this time I was very weak, my mouth was dry as a bone and I was seriously considering getting stuck into my last water bottle. Croukamp decided, despite objections from Wilson and me, to make for the Limpopo river with every empty water bottle he could carry and then return to our position. This would entail a round trip of approximately forty kilometres. By this time I felt as if I

THE OPERATION THAT WENT WRONG

was floating on air due to the fatigue and dehydration. Perhaps Wilson and I should have tried to physically stop Croukamp from going, but when this man has made his mind up, nothing on this earth will change it. What he did was against all standard operating procedures, he made the decision when he was dehydrated and his thinking was unclear. We did not see him for another week or so until we had returned to Rhodesia.

That night the clouds opened and the rain pelted down all night. Wilson and I made shelters with our groundsheets and collected water. We were able to fill all the water bottles we still had and I filled my plastic water bag as well. Strangely, I had trouble drinking more than one mug of water, although I thought I would be able to drink at least a gallon. At first light on Sunday we stood to, made our first brew of tea and had a good feed. Sunday passed with no sign of the column or any movement on the road or railway line. We still thought our position was as intended, some 100 kilometres from the Rhodesian border, and passed this on to HQ in our situation reports. The column had been delayed after its entry into Mozambique and, unbeknown to us, was to be twenty-four hours late in picking us up. Sunday dragged on and on and still there was no sign of the column. We kept one of the small means, a VHF personal radio, on listening watch, hoping to hear the armoured column coming to pick us up.

By Monday morning, Wilson and I were getting worried. We contacted base on the big means, our VHF radio, gave them the grid reference of the location where we thought we were and were told to await uplift. We waited all of Monday, and it seemed like an age. Then late, very late on Monday afternoon we heard our call sign on the small means. It was very faint, but it was definitely somebody calling us. We replied but they couldn't hear us. About fifteen minutes later we heard our call sign once again. We replied and this time made contact with a single vehicle from the column, which confirmed that they were on the way to pick us up. What joy, what relief.

Thirty minutes later a 'Pig', a locally made armoured personnel carrier based on a Mercedes Unimog 2.5-ton chassis, rattled into view along the dirt road at the side of the railway line. We wasted no time getting on board, turning around, and heading north back to the column, after explaining why Croukamp was missing. Lieutenant Passaportis, who commanded the Pig, explained to us that we were at least forty kilometres south of our reported position, which was confusing to say the least.

After rendezvousing with the other vehicles, we returned to Rhodesia

Selous Scouts Mercedes Unimog 2.5 truck, 1976. *Photo* Dennis Croukamp

Selous Scouts column gets a visit from 7 Squadron RhAF. *Photo* Dennis Croukamp

several days later. After many adventures and many days, Croukamp finally walked back into Rhodesia, near 'Crooks Corner', where the borders of Rhodesia, South Africa and Mozambique meet.

I believe I have the answer to why we were dropped forty kilometres south and sixty kilometres east of our intended drop zone.

During the Second World War bombers returning from high-altitude operations over Germany often returned much faster than anticipated. At the time the reasons for this were not understood. After the war, it was found that at high altitudes there are often very strong winds, now known as the 'jet stream'. In the northern hemisphere these winds blow from east to west and in the southern hemisphere they blow from west to east, often in excess of 100 mph.

The case of the British South American Airways Lancastrian aircraft, Stardust, which crashed into the Andes in South America in 1947, illustrates this effect. On a trip from Buenos Aires in Argentina to Santiago in Peru, in thick cloud conditions, the aircraft was navigating on time-and-distance dead reckoning in thick cloud conditions. When the crew thought they were fifty miles from Santiago, they began their descent from the cruising altitude of 24,000 feet and crashed into one of the highest peaks in the Andes. In fact, they were some 100 miles east of their predicted position and had been flying into a headwind from the northwest in excess of 100 mph, which they were unaware of. A similar wind, in our case a tailwind from the northwest, must have affected our dead-reckoning run after dropping Lieutenant S and his colleague.

On return to Salisbury, there was no debrief from any of the officers and there was no attempt to apply 'lessons learned'. Any professional soldier will tell you that the most important aspect of any operation is the debrief. There were many lessons learned from this operation:

1. Never go into the bush until you are perfectly bush fit
2. Never believe what anyone tells you about a target until you have seen a photograph of it and seen the target … and even touched it
3. What can go wrong will go wrong: plan accordingly
4. Remember the seven Ps: Prior Preparation and Planning Prevent Piss-Poor Performance.

That march was just as hard as, or perhaps even harder than, any 'long drag' I have done on any selection course. After that operation, all the others were easy. I like working for organizations that are well organized, slick and professional. After yet another badly organized adventure, I moved on to one of the pseudo troops. This was run by a long-service senior infantry NCO, which was much more to my liking.

5

Anecdotes

An unusual tracking follow-up
Dennis Croukamp and I were in the Selous Scouts fort at Chiredzi sometime late in 1976. The fort was empty except for us, the fort commander, Major S, the air liaison officer Squadron Leader 'Frantan' Fenton-Wells and the usual admin people. The Special Branch people were not there nor were their black police assistants, which was a bit unusual.

    Dennis and I had been in the air force bar the previous evening so we were a bit hung over. Major S took a phone call from the nearby army camp which had a Territorial Force element there at the time. I think it was 4th Battalion Rhodesia Regiment. These people were all civvies doing compulsory six-week call-ups. The TFs wanted to know if the Scouts fort had any trackers available for an immediate follow-up south of Chiredzi near the Lundi river on the edge of the Lunde Tribal Trust Land. A bridge over the Lundi River had been attacked the previous night and there were fresh tracks to follow.

    Major S volunteered Dennis and me for the job. Unfortunately, we only had terrorist equipment with us so we had to borrow a couple of FN rifles, jump into the waiting Alouette III chopper and get off to the 4th Battalion headquarters about 30 minutes' flying time from the fort. We were both in army shirts, shorts, black anti-tracking 'takkies' (canvas ankle boots with smooth rubber soles) and belt webbing containing water, two days' rations, some ammunition and small VHF radios with a range of about three kilometres on flat ground.

    When we landed at the HQ we were met by the company commander and another TF officer.

    The tented camp was in a very pleasant position, well shaded and with a generator running, so they were quite comfortable. The camp guards, however, were all ancient men and I wondered who would be the follow-up troops for our tracking team. The OC could probably see the look on my face and immediately said, "Don't worry; you will be working with one of our very best call signs. All fit young men." This was reassuring.

    After a quick study of the map, we emplaned in our waiting chopper and flew off to the bridge. As soon as we had landed, the Alouette III returned to

Chiredzi as we looked around for our follow-up troops. Four young white TF lads came out of the tree line and approached us. We expected more … at least twenty.

Normally a combat tracker team (CTT) comprises four trained trackers: tracker leader, two flankers and the tracker controller at the rear. They work in a diamond formation with the lead tracker at the front, the two flankers on each side covering him, and with the controller at the rear maintaining communications with the follow-up troops (FUTs) behind. The FUTs would ideally be trained infantry in platoon strength, between twenty and forty men. The lead tracker keeps his eyes on the ground and looks for spoor and sign. Spoor is anything at ground level, like marks or shiny patches, and sign is anything above ground level, like flattened grass or bent branches. This is a very tiring job and the lead tracker is usually changed every half an hour or so. The flankers cover the tracker and protect him. If the tracker loses spoor then the flankers and the tracker cast for spoor, which means walking round in increasing circles until you find something. Whoever picks up some sign or spoor becomes the new lead tracker. The tracker controller at the rear controls the operation and informs the FUTs' platoon commander. It is also his job to hurry them up if they lag behind, which often happens in thick bush or difficult country.

With only two trackers and four FUTs we would be hard-pressed if we blundered into a large group of terrorists. However, our four TF chums seemed enthusiastic and gave us a quick overview of the situation. They were armed exactly as we were and in addition carried a TR48 HF radio which had a range of several hundred kilometres.

The bridge was a new reinforced concrete structure over the Lundi and carried a road of compacted gravel about twenty feet wide. To the north was white farming land and to the south the Lundi Tribal Trust Land. The Lundi TTL was a large expanse of land inhabited by Shona-speaking African families grouped in villages or family settlements and cultivating the land on a subsistence basis. About half a mile south of the bridge was a group of coloured (mixed race) protection company troops looking after some bulldozers and graders used for building the new road.

Early the previous evening a group of approximately twenty ZANLA terrorists had arrived, walking down the road from the direction of the TTL and dragging a recoilless rifle behind them. A recoilless rifle is a big gun that fires shells and this one was either Russian or Chinese and mounted on a two-wheeled carriage for easy transportation. The terrorists had fired several shells from the riverbank at the bridge at a range of about 100 metres. They had damaged the structure only slightly and had left several empty cases behind on the bank. The cases positively identified the weapon as a Chinese 76mm recoilless rifle. The cases are made of brass, about three foot in height, similar to a big rifle bullet but with holes in them. We asked one of the protection company troops why they had not collected the empty cases.

"Oh, we thought they were bulldozer filters or something like that," they replied.

Hmm. These guys were obviously not very motivated and didn't give a damn. No doubt they had melted away when the gooks arrived.

Without wasting any time, we set off on spoor along the road following the wheel marks in the dust. After a kilometre or so, the marks headed off the road across country. The spoor here was for approximately fourteen men. Several were heavily loaded, so they must have been carrying the recoilless rifle ammunition. The spoor was easy to follow at this stage as the drag marks were prominent and easily identified. Shortly after leaving the road, the spoor diverged. The drag marks made by the wheels then stopped. Six men went one way and the rest of the group went another. They were anti-tracking, which is the term used when one covers ones tracks or 'bombshells' into singles or pairs in order to throw off one's pursuers. We followed the marks of the group with the heaviest load. They were manhandling the gun. By late afternoon we hit a prominent cut line through the bush and stopped to cast for spoor as we had lost it momentarily.

At that point we heard the faint sound of motorcycles approaching. Then we heard an unknown call sign calling us on our VHF radios. This call sign was a Rhodesian army experimental motorcycle unit that had recently been formed to assist in tracking, convoy escorts and so on. They rode 350cc Suzuki motorbikes that had been effectively silenced and carried cut-down FN rifles on clips on the handlebars. They had been sent to assist. After a short chat, we each jumped on the back of a bike and set off down the cut line cutting for spoor.

My driver was an American and he several times looked over his shoulder at me and shouted, "We're making history man!" He was cheerfully enthusiastic.

It was so much easier than walking and we found the drag marks of the wheels very quickly. This would have taken hours had we been on foot. We stayed on the bikes until just before dark when the motorcycles had to leave.

By this time we were deep inside the Lundi TTL.

Just after the bikes left us the spoor disappeared. The terrorists had walked a herd of cows over the tracks. In addition, all the kraals and the fields around us were deserted. These were warning signs that we were closing in on the terrorists. We cast for spoor and found a lot of suspicious spoor in a nearby kraal. The village had only very recently been abandoned, maybe in just the last half hour. A cooking fire was still burning and there were a number of pots of *ropoco*, a stiff porridge made from millet, around the edge of the fire. We quickly estimated the population of the kraal by the number of beds in the huts and it was apparent that far more food had been prepared than was necessary for the number of people in such a small village. This kraal was feeding terrorists and we were about thirty minutes behind them.

As darkness fell we split up into pairs, took pots of food and some blankets which were airing over a nearby bush and slept in pairs near the kraal. If we had stayed in a group we would have needed to put out a sentry while we slept. Sleeping in pairs has the advantage that one does not have to put out a sentry. The risk of the enemy walking onto two people is small. However, I was in favour of not splitting the group and carrying out surveillance on the village. I was overruled.

Come morning, we rendezvoused at a prearranged spot and as a group we took stock of the situation. We decided to check out the kraal and if we found no sign of the terrorists or any civilians, we would withdraw from the TTL and request uplift.

We moved carefully towards the kraal which was still deserted and cast for spoor. There was nothing fresh. Nobody had been back in the night. It was a dead end. We moved toward the nearest tarred road and called for uplift. A truck arrived to take us back to the TF base where we dropped off the FUTs before Dennis and I headed back to the Scouts fort at Chiredzi.

While this job was a bit of a 'lemon', that is, it went sour on us, it kept up the pressure on the terrorists. The motorbikes had been useful. I believe if we had got hold of the motorbikes an hour earlier we might have caught up with the enemy. Nine out of ten tracking follow-ups do not produce a result either due to the terrorists' anti-tracking or spoor and sign being lost through weather and wind dissipating the marks. However Combat Tracking Teams were, and still are today, a valuable tool in counter-insurgency operations.

How Captain Gillespie almost started an international incident

Captain Gillespie, brother of Lieutenant Gillespie of the Rhodesian SAS, was based at the Selous Scouts fort at Chiredzi as the operations officer. He was also a practised practical joker. One of the other whites based at the fort was Squadron Leader 'Frantan' Fenton-Wells who was both the air liaison officer and the butt of several of Gillespie's jokes.

One day Gillespie enlisted the help of one of the Blues helicopter pilots and a Special Branch colleague to play a special joke. The next day, an Alouette III helicopter hovered above the Scouts fort and slowly descended into the courtyard. Gillespie unlocked the door of the ammo store and helped the storeman take out four mortar-bomb boxes that were packed with plastic explosives in readiness for a forthcoming job. On cue, the SB man came out of his office with his pack and his machine pistol and began helping load the boxes onto the chopper which had landed with the rotors still turning.

Frantan rushed out of the ops room and shouted across to Gillespie, "I haven't ordered up a chopper. What are you up to?"

"Don't worry," Gillespie replied, "we're only going across to Mozambique to take out a pylon on the power line." The power line in question ran from the hydroelectric plant at Cabora Bassa dam in Tete province, Mozambique to South Africa. "That way we'll interrupt the power supply to South Africa and bring them into the war," the SB man chipped in.

"You can't do that! It hasn't been authorized. You've got no authority: it's illegal," Frantan pleaded as the chopper lifted off and disappeared in the direction of the border. Immediately Frantan disappeared into the ops room and phoned everybody he could think of, including air headquarters at Combined Operations in Salisbury. Finally he went across to the Blues compound.

"Do you know what Gillespie and that chopper pilot are up to?" he demanded.

"Yes," said the duty officer. "It's supposed to be a test flight but they've really gone to lunch at the sugar mill club."

Frantan had been 'had' in a big way, and Gillespie received a huge 'rocket'!

How the troop commander tried to shoot his foot off

The Selous Scout troop I was in comprised around forty black soldiers, both turned terrorists and enlisted soldiers, as well as two whites. After a four-week deployment, the troop returned to the Scouts fort at Chiredzi for a few days' rest before another two-week deployment into a Tribal Trust Land.

That evening, after the troop had been fed and debriefed by Special Branch, the troop commander, Pete, and I got into some clean clothes and headed into the town with some other Scouts also passing through the fort. After some time at the local pub, we all climbed back into the truck and headed back for the fort. In the morning as we were breakfasting, I noticed that Pete was not with us. Someone else also noticed his absence and after a brief discussion, the realization dawned that we must have left him in the pub. Some minutes later the bell on the front gate of the fort rang and in walked the warrant officer. "You naughty boys, you left me behind," he said, or words to that effect.

Now Pete always carried a Tokarev pistol in a leather holster on his belt. The Tokarev is a cheaply made Soviet pistol with virtually no safety devices but with very powerful ammunition. Pete invariably kept one round 'up the spout' when he left the fort and usually unloaded on returning. However, in his haste to chastise us for leaving him behind, he had forgotten to unload. Before sitting down, he loosened his belt and made to take it off. The leather holster slid from the belt and fell off. Then everything went into slow motion: the holster slowly rotated as it fell to the concrete floor, pistol hammer first, as Pete raised one foot to stop the holster's fall. Simultaneously, everyone took steps, big ones, backwards. As the hammer hit the ground, a round went off and Pete's foot was directly in line with the muzzle of the pistol. The bullet passed through the flesh between the first two toes of his foot and then through the roof of the fort. The wound kept Pete out of the bush for a month and was extremely painful and inconvenient.

Lessons learned:
1. Don't miss the bus
2. Always unload when you enter a fort!

The trooper who could (not) speak Shona

A Shona language course had been organized by Philippa Berlyn, a local journalist, author and linguist in Salisbury, for some SAS troopies, in order for them to learn the basics of the language. They were a lazy lot and spent most of the time lounging around Philippa's pool rather than grafting away at their studies. Philippa was highly knowledgeable about the Shona language and customs. I once saw her correct the grammar of some Shona troops on the Scouts selection course I did. The SAS troopies on the Shona course returned to the unit and went back onto ops. Shortly thereafter, some terrorists were holed up in a cave and were proving difficult to extricate. An officer, Lieutenant

Warraker, said, "Lance-Corporal D, you've done the Shona course. Tell these guys to come out with their hands up."

Lance-Corporal D stood up and shouted out in English, "Come out with your hands up." He hadn't learned a single word of Shona …

Don't worry; it's only a bang and a whoosh

By 1978 there was a need for Scouts pseudo-troops to mark targets for Fire Force assaults at ranges up to 3,000 metres. The hand-held commando mortar was only good for firing smoke up to 1,500 metres so there was a clear need for a new target-marking system.

The Scouts white RSM called my troop commander and me over to the range one morning where the engineers were about to demonstrate a new target-marking system. Also at the range was Major S, who screwed two aluminium tubes together and handed them to Pete, my troop commander. I thought to myself, "Why doesn't S demo this himself?" I was to find out later.

The RSM slid a SNEB 60mm aircraft rocket into the end of the tube and said to Pete, "Don't worry, it just goes with a bang and a *whoosh*. Press this button and off she goes … should be good for up to 3,000 metres."

It looked a real Heath Robinson contraption, so I stood well back. So did Major S and the RSM. That should have told me something.

Pete took aim down the range and pressed the button. There was the most enormous bang, clouds of smoke and Pete was sitting on his arse, as the rocket disappeared skyward. That was the last we saw of the new target-marking system.

Anybody want to get rid of a ton of explosive?

Captain Charlie Small of the Rhodesian Engineers went on several external operations with Scouts, destroying bridges and other structures with commercial explosive. After one operation, there was a ton of commercial explosive left over which was in an unstable state, leaking greasy liquid from the cardboard cartons it was packed in. Charlie offered to give 6 Troop a lesson in demolition techniques, which was very good of him. Using the 6 Troop Mercedes 4.5-ton truck, we loaded the highly unstable explosive and took it to where Charlie wanted to blow it up. I thought we should have gone farther away but Charlie seemed to think 300 metres from Main Camp was all right. We loaded the cartons into a depression in the ground ringed by trees and set up two ring mains of cordtex detonating cord and two initiating

Charlie Small (Rhodesian Engineers). *Photo* Dennis Croukamp

sets comprising pull igniters and extremely short lengths of fuse instantaneous. Charlie seemed to think it was sufficient. Personally, I would have liked longer fuses. Charlie got two black soldiers to pull the igniters as we hopped on the truck and drove off.

The bang was immense. We could feel the pressure wave inside the truck cab. I knew then that there would be trouble. I said to Charlie, "Did you tell anyone about this?" He just shook his head and grinned, which confirmed to me that there would be trouble. The RSM was really angry. Inkomo Camp went onto alert because they thought there was a terrorist attack under way. Main Camp lost some windows and all the trees around the depression were flattened. Sadly Charlie was killed later when the Puma helicopter he was in crashed in Mozambique.

How do these sights work?

After one Scouts external op, a number of 76mm recoilless rifles and ammunition were recovered back to the Selous Scouts camp at Inkomo. These weapons were wheeled breech-loading guns with the capability of firing either high explosive (HE) or anti-tank armour-piercing (AP) rounds and had two sets of sights. Nobody had used them before. Captain Rob Warraker asked 6 Troop to take one of the guns to the range with some HE and AP rounds to test them out. This was a case of the blind leading the blind. Warraker aimed the gun at a target 1,500 metres away as we loaded an AP round and Warraker lined up the sights. It was a simple job to cock the mechanism and pull the trigger. The round sailed off high into the sky and disappeared into the far distance in the direction of a farm.

"Clearly," said Warraker, "that was the HE sight and I fired an AP round."

We packed up quickly and scuttled off back to camp before anyone could complain.

Lesson learned: know the difference between the ammunition and the sights before you pop a round off.

The armoured bus

The bus in question was captured by a Selous Scouts armoured column during an external operation in Mozambique, which also saw the 'liberation' of a road grader. The bus was then painted in the colours of the Shu Shine Bus Company, armoured with sheet metal on the sides, rear and front and fitted with twin MAG machine guns on the roof and rear. The workshops then rewired the bus, ready for 6 Troop to use. The idea was to take it into the southeast Tribal Trust Lands to look for bands of gooks who were robbing buses. This sounded easy, but things started to go wrong even before we left Main Camp.

We loaded up the bus at Inkomo and headed off to the Chiredzi area. I sat on my tin barrack box behind our driver as the troop commander, Pete, went into 'eyelid-inspection' mode at the rear. As we approached the camp gate, we went over a bump in the road. The windscreen shattered and the night air was punctuated by a burst of machine-gun fire. "Attack", I thought. However, the real reason was a worn sear on an RPD machine gun: the lance-corporal seated behind me had cocked his weapon as we left the vehicle park and had placed the weapon on the floor, resting on the bipod. The bump had fired the weapon, which drilled the box I was seated on. The rounds bounced off the metal sheet on my right and deflected through the windscreen, narrowly missing the driver. I had nearly been shot in the arse and Pete got woken up.

One day while touring the southeast Tribal Trust Lands, travelling rapidly down a steep incline, the driver started waving the steering wheel at me: it had come off. The bus lurched from side to side on the narrow road and I had a sense of impending doom as our momentum increased. You won't believe this, but the bus ran off the road onto the only flat bit of ground for miles and slowed gracefully to a halt with minimum damage.

The next day, we were out until dark so the driver switched on the lights. The sidelights were fine. When it got really dark, on went the headlamps; however, when the driver pressed the dip switch, every bit of wiring began to incinerate. The control panel lit up cherry red with smoke billowing all over the bus. Clearly, there was a short circuit somewhere. However, all was not lost. Very slowly, we made our way back to camp by the light of a pocket torch. A friendly auto-electrician fixed the wiring and, unfortunately, we were soon back on the road.

The bus was so heavy it couldn't go uphill with all the kit and people we had on board. Everybody had to get off and walk behind while Pete poured water into the boiling radiator. When passing bus stops, we were unable to stop to pick up passengers. I have vivid memories of crowds of irate Africans running down the road after our Shu Shine bus, waving and screaming at us to stop.

And we failed to contact any bus robbers. What a disaster.

The vertically challenged OC

The Officer Commanding C Squadron Rhodesian SAS at the time was vertically challenged and highly conscious of the fact. He occupied an office at Cranborne barracks which had a wooden door with both a brass door handle and a letterbox. One dark night, a practical joker unscrewed the handle and the letterbox and fixed them at the bottom of the door about six inches off the floor. And then the coward went on leave! In the morning the OC turned up for work to find his redesigned door accoutrements at the height only a midget would use. He went ballistic and searched high and low for the culprit to no avail. I cannot tell a lie: it was Dave Scales.

I bet I can … I bet you can't

As a civilian in Salisbury I knew a few soldiers, mainly from the skydiving scene, and one of them, Dave Scales – our occasional door furniture technician! – was a corporal in SAS. The middle of any week was usually a bit boring so when he invited me to the SAS corporals' club, the Winged Stagger, for a quiet drink one Wednesday, it seemed a good idea. That night after a few beers, the discussion turned to selection courses and we compared notes on the ones we had each done: he on the Rhodesian course and me on the British course. Inevitably, we started on the "My course was harder than your course" routine.

Dave challenged me, "I bet you couldn't pass our course." to which I replied

"I could piss all over your course," I replied. After that many drinks inside me I was bulletproof.

"I bet you couldn't," he said.

"I bet you I could," I replied.

"There's one soon; why don't you try it?" was his retort.

That didn't stop me because I was invulnerable, at least until the next morning. When I awoke with a hangover, I knew immediately that I would look silly if I didn't do the course.

So, with an aching head I popped down to the army recruiting office and signed on the dotted line for three years.

About 2 weeks later the survivors of the selection course arrived back at Cranborne barracks. We unloaded our kit from the lorry and I went to look for Dave to give him the news. I found him packing his gear.

"Where are you off to? I asked.

"Greece, for two whole weeks."

"Oh lovely," I said.

I did not know at that time but the OC had offered anyone who introduced a candidate to the unit two weeks' leave if his recruit passed selection.

"Bye bye," said Dave. "See you when I get back."

I had been 'had'.

How we got lost, a warrant officer had a ride on an ambulance trolley and I nearly squashed the quartermaster

In 1981 the entire 6 Reconnaissance Commando, South African Defence Force, was warned for an operation in Mozambique. We were to attack three ANC houses in the Maputo suburb of Matola. This would be achieved by entering Maputo in a column of vehicles which would then split into three smaller groups. Each house would be neutralized by house-clearing teams wearing body armour and helmets and armed with folding-butt AK-47 rifles with seventy-five-round drum magazines. The column would reform after the operation and return to South Africa on exactly the same route in the early hours of the following morning. Drivers had night-vision goggles and vehicle lights were banned.

Any soldier will tell you that going in and coming out on the same route

Author with Magirus Deutz truck in South Africa before deployment into Mozambique, 1980.

The rear of my Magirus Deutz truck. Before deployment into Mozambique, 1980.

is asking for trouble.

The vehicles we were to use were a mix of Mercedes 2.5-ton Unimogs and Magirus Deutz 10-ton trucks. The Unimogs were relatively nimble but the Deutz trucks were slow and required a large turning circle. The Magirus Deutz which I drove was governed to 55 kph, and had a 'crash' gearbox: it required a sympathetic driver to operate the gears without crashing them and it was very slow to accelerate due to the large amount of sandbags, armour plate, 20mm cannon, mortar tube, ten men with body armour, weapons and personal kit on the back. The rear of the truck was protected with armour plate and sandbags but the cab was unprotected. Consequently, if we took fire from the front and I was immobilized then the truck would come to a stop. These vehicles were totally wrong for this job.

The column was to travel 'covertly' from Durban but the column still looked like regular army trucks with tarpaulins covering 20mm cannons and recoilless rifles. It was not a covert journey in any way. The lead truck, containing the squadron commander, the only person who knew the final destination (big security here!), was the fastest truck and the last truck was the slowest with an engine governed to 55 kph. Well, it didn't take long for the convoy to become hopelessly strung out along the road to Johannesburg and for the 'small means' in the rear truck to lose communications with the lead truck.

A recipe for disaster you might think? Not for the resourceful lads of 6 Recce Cdo. We stopped at a filling station in Harrismith and bought a road map of South Africa. Lieutenant Cole had overheard the OC say that the destination "begins with a 'K'". We pored over the map, scrutinizing all the places beginning with 'K'. Was it 'Kaapstaad'? … No, too far … 'Kokstad'? … No, not there either … It must be 'Komatipoort' … Yes, that must be it! So off we went to Komatipoort on the Mozambican border.

Was this an omen of things to come? Yes.

We found some of our lads waiting for us on the side of the road on the way to Komatipoort and followed them to the 'security-sterile' area from where the attack would be launched. In the camp were signals tents with women working telex machines and army colonels in uniform driving in and out of the camp in bright yellow civilian Toyota Corolla cars—with radio antennas ten feet long mounted on the rear bumpers. In no way was this a security-sterile area.

The proposed route across country to the main Maputo road was an old wagon route that had been walked over by a reconnaissance party. The recce team had underestimated the time required for the column to travel the few kilometres on this very old track. Consequently, we were several hours late reaching the main tar road on the outskirts of Maputo and so turned back after reaching the first road sign saying 'Maputo'. On the return journey along the old wagon road one of our number, a large warrant officer called Johnny, who was in the Unimog in front of my truck, had been sitting in the truck for hours wearing body armour, belt webbing and chest webbing. He stood up to stretch his legs. At that very moment the truck passed under a low branch which propelled Johnny off the back of the truck and onto the ground. Judging by his screams, he had seriously hurt his back. His comrades on the truck awkwardly clambered down due to all the gear they were trussed up in and finally managed to get Johnny back on the vehicle.

Was this an omen? Yes.

The entry into South Africa was through the barbed-wire fence that marked the international boundary. We made a sharp left turn onto the border road to our security-sterile camp. Now, it's a strange thing that when every vehicle in a convoy makes a turn, the next truck behind usually cuts the corner just a little bit sharper than the vehicle in front. Our convoy was no exception. Our quartermaster, Captain Simmons, a resourceful former Royal Marine, was waiting for us at the border crossing with his rifle, 'small means' VHF radio and a torch to see us safely through. He was standing on the inside of the 'turn' with his back to the barbed-wire fence against a very stout wooden post. He signalled with his torch to each vehicle to make a left turn onto the border road. What with the dust from all the vehicles, the pitch-black night, my tiredness and the sharp turn, all I remember is seeing him disappear, or so it seemed to me, under the back wheels of my truck. The torch illuminated his face like a spectre in a horror movie. He said something that sounded like "Aargh!" I really thought I'd killed him.

I remarked to Pete Cole, in the passenger seat of the truck, "I think I've just squashed the QM." At which Pete curled up laughing and disappeared onto the floor of the cab in convulsions of mirth. I just want to say sorry to the QM for giving him a rifle that could shoot round corners, a flat profile 'small means' (radio set), barbed-wire scratches and for laughing at his predicament. But it was very funny at the time.

The warrant officer with the injured back was loaded onto an ambulance and taken to the local airfield where a plane would fly him to hospital in Durban. Sadly, the ambulance crew in Durban that collected him at the airport lacked a degree of professionalism. They put him on a wheeled trolley and loaded him in the back of the vehicle but forgot to lock the doors. On the journey to hospital the doors flew open and the trolley sped off down the road like something out of a Keystone Cops movie. Oh how we all laughed. I collapsed with laughter when I finally got home and told my wife.

The bad news was that the job had to be done again. I missed the operation this time round because my wife was due to give birth to our first child. The same column took the same route in and the same route out. Sadly, at the house my team was tasked to neutralize they took three dead and five wounded. Otherwise it was a success, but at a cost in irreplaceable men. Lessons learned were several:
1. Choose nimble, agile vehicles with enough speed to get you out of trouble and with a small turning circle
2. Don't take the same route in and the same route out
3. Travel at night to the firm base in a disciplined convoy with good communications between all vehicles
4. Ensure the firm base is properly security-sterile: no one comes in and no one goes out
5. Don't stand on the inside of a corner.

We had learned all these lessons in Rhodesia but they were either not remembered or were not implemented.

Captain Gillespie – more practical joking!
The Scouts fort at Chiredzi was mighty hot in the summer and flies were a problem. Aerosol cans of fly spray were left around the place. Captain G had the jolly wheeze of replacing the label on a can of white spray paint with the label from a can of fly spray. After a jolly night at the Blues pub on the airfield, Bunny Hardt, our vehicle mechanic, and I repaired to our beds. Bunny went into anti-fly mode and liberally sprayed the corners of the room, his bed, his stomach, his back and other areas with 'fly spray'. In the morning we wondered why everything, including Bunny, was painted white. Captain G had been at work.

How some enemy had an uplifting experience
One of the first operations I ever did was a road ambush in Mozambique. A Troop of C Squadron (Rhodesian) SAS was based in a bush camp in the eastern districts near the Tanganda Tea Estate. The estate had been having

trouble with ZANLA terrorists and Frelimo soldiers coming across the border and intimidating and robbing estate workers. In addition, ZANLA was using this area as an infiltration route. Special Branch had intelligence that a specific road to the border was being used to transport the terrorists, where they would be dropped off before crossings into Rhodesia on foot. The plan was for a column of SAS, about twenty operators, to make a night approach march onto the road where a long-term ambush would be established.

My call sign of four people, was commanded by Ian Suttill, ex-Royal Marines. I packed ten days' rations into my rucksack with five days' water, 600 rounds of ammunition for my AK-47 rifle, grenades, lightweight sleeping bag, groundsheet and Australian bivouac sheet. The column had two TR48 high-frequency radios, one with the column commander's call sign and the other carried by me. It was a bulky radio but it was a highly effective transmitter/receiver in both voice and Morse operation with an excellent range. It was far better than anything in use by British Special Forces at that time. The column also carried several Soviet TM46 anti-tank mines with kit for laying them and for remote detonation. Each mine contained 5.6kgs of TNT in a metal case and was designed to activate by a weight depressing the centre of the casing. One of these mines could stop any truck.

The column was dropped off by truck late one afternoon close to the border. When night fell we crossed the border fence, a four-strand wire fence about four feet high, and marched into Mozambique in single file. After marching the entire night, the column halted shortly before dawn near the road, which was a compacted dirt and gravel road about twenty feet wide. It was well made with drainage ditches both sides. A firm base was established and clearance patrols were sent up and down the road to clear the area and search for a suitable ambush position. The patrol returned to report that the only tracks on the road were old bicycle spoor. So much for this being a well-used road. They also reported that the terrain was as flat as a billiard table, that there were no signs of any human habitation and that this location was as good a place as any from which to ambush any vehicles.

We settled down to a long-term ambush. One patrol of four went 'up' the road and another went 'down' the road, to act as stop groups or early warning groups and were in touch with the main ambush group of twelve operators by VHF radio. The main ambush party or 'killer group' dug in two remotely detonated TM46 mines, which would be electrically detonated by the ambush commander.

And then it rained continuously for thirty-six hours. It was very wet and cold. We could only move away from the ambush position once a day for a hot drink and some food. However, after forty-eight hours or so, a message came through on the radio that several Frelimo soldiers were coming down the road looking for spoor. I watched them arrive at our location. They were walking along quite slowly with two in front and two some way behind. The men in front were being very conscientious, examining the entire width of the road for spoor, or marks at ground level. The rain was both good news and bad news. Good news because any sign or spoor made by digging in the mines and the detonating cable would have been obliterated; bad news because the rain would have disturbed the soil over the mines, which was looser than the surrounding dirt road and thus more obvious. The first Frelimo soldier, who must have been the leader, was slowly walking to where the first mine had been dug in. He paused and went on. Then he turned and went back. He called his colleague across and they both studied the spot where the mine was buried. They then called to their two comrades about fifty metres behind them and the four of them began peering down. The leader was pointing down at the road and said something. Then his pal said something and pointed into the bush where we were and then pointed down at the road where the mine was and said something more. The leader seemed to agree and they all looked down. The leader rubbed the soil off the top of the mine with his boot. They all looked down. Then they all looked into the bush as the leader used his boot to rub away more soil.

Then the mine went *BANG* with dirt and dust rising high into the air. There was nothing left of the Frelimo soldiers.

Ian Suttill fell about laughing and we all laughed like drains. It was like something out of a movie. But it was the end of the ambush: our position was now compromised. We waited around until nightfall but no one came looking for four missing Frelimo soldiers. That night we packed up and headed for home and debriefs.

How a friend had parachute malfunctions on two consecutive parachute jumps and more besides

The first half of this story is set in the Rhodesian SAS in 1978 and the second half in the South African Reconnaissance Commandos in 1980. I did not see the first part of this tale because I was in Selous Scouts at the time, but I did see the second. The circumstances of the first part were described to me by someone who watched it all unfold.

A friend of mine in the Rhodesian SAS was involved in a 'blue on blue' or friendly-fire incident in which an SAS soldier, Dick Beiderman, died. Sometime later the SAS was tasked for a camp attack and my friend was in the static-line parachute wave. I'll cut things short and just say that he had a total malfunction on his main canopy. He got his reserve out but because we jumped from very low altitudes it only partially inflated before he crashed through some trees which broke his fall. However, he did injure his back and was off work for a while.

The black humour emerged once again with everyone telling him: "Dick failed that time but he'll get you the next time you jump."

My pal vowed never to jump again. He left the unit shortly afterwards and worked for the police.

We lost the war in Rhodesia and the South African Defence Force employed a lot of SAS guys in 6 Recce Commando based in Durban. My friend came with us but when one is a 'Recce' one has to parachute. If one doesn't, then one cannot stay in the Recces. Simple.

The whole unit went off to Zululand, near St Lucia along the North Coast from Durban, to do a refresher static-line parachute course. We used South African Air Force DC-3 aircraft and jumped with steerable round parachutes. From an altitude of about 800 feet, we parachuted on some very flat land that was springy, soft sand with a few pine trees and isolated clumps of salt-tolerant bush. I was on the first aircraft and jumped uneventfully. After landing, I collected up my kit and walked towards the truck to load my gear on it. I turned and watched the next aircraft run in and drop the second load. The third or fourth man to jump had a total parachute malfunction on his main canopy. The canopy came off his back and 'Roman candled' as they called it in the Second World War. After what seemed a long time but was probably just a few seconds, the parachutist pulled his reserve parachute mounted on his belly. Instead of throwing the main parachute away from him he did nothing. The reserve parachute slowly wrapped itself around the streaming main all the way to the top and then slowly began to unwind as it lazily began to inflate. Then the guy hit some bushes and bounced. I clearly saw daylight between him and the ground. I thought he was dead.

Amazingly, the ground was so soft that he survived. It was my pal on his second parachute malfunction on consecutive jumps! He was in Addington hospital in Durban in a flash and after a month on his back was back at work. It is statistically impossible for anyone in the world to have total canopy malfunctions on consecutive jumps. It never ever happens. But it did in this case.

Was Dick involved?

Poor old Bates

I just want to say sorry to Albert 'Bates' Maré, a strapping Afrikaans lad in the Rhodesian SAS, whose English was not too perfect. This was why he couldn't complain fast enough when Ian Suttill designated him to carry the MAG belt-fed machine gun and a ton of ammunition. Let me explain why I want to apologize.

The squadron had been deployed in the eastern districts at a tea plantation near Tanganda which had suffered terrorist incursions and disruption to production in late 1975. It was our job to cross the border into Mozambique in a show of force and check out various terrorist locations. Getting over the border entailed crossing a small river which was the international boundary on the edge of the tea plantation. A skinny, little tree had been felled across the river to use as a bridge by some person or persons who did not realize that a column of forty soldiers, all armed to the teeth, would strain the little tree to its limits. Crossing the river was fine for the first few sticks of four men. The sapling was slightly springy but by the time the last stick came to cross, the tree had some serious bounce in it. Ian Suttill got over fine just as the tree made a cracking sound like that of an AK round, which split the dark night like a knife, boding ill for the final three shivering in the chill of the night. Next across was Dave who sprinted over. I went next to the accompaniment of more cracks and some huge oscillations from the tree trunk.

Last to cross was 'Bates'. He was armed to the teeth with the MAG, 600 rounds and all the other kit. He was a big lad; his total weight must have been in the region of 300 pounds. Sadly the little tree surrendered to the 300-pound trooper and with an almighty crack gave up the struggle. Splash went Bates into the river and everyone burst out laughing. Ian laughed so much he fell over and rolled around hugging his stomach. We were laughing so much that 'Bates' had to get out of the river by himself. So much for our clandestine entry.

I just wanted to say sorry for laughing, Bates. But it was funny.

Frantan kept his head while others lost theirs

In early 1976 I was at the Selous Scouts fort at Chiredzi waiting for 6 Troop to arrive so I could go on ops with them. Major S, the fort commander, was tasked to take a twenty-man ambush group about thirty kilometres into Mozambique to ambush the road that ran alongside the railway line from Maputo to Malvernia on the Rhodesian border. ZANLA terrorists used the railway to deploy their men to the Rhodesian border. The line had been destroyed in several places so they took the train as far as they could then deployed on foot on the dirt road that ran alongside the line. Specific intelligence indicated a large terrorist group would be moving along the road in a short while.

Major S liked gadgets so he designed and made the world's biggest claymore mine for this job. A claymore is a small anti-personnel mine, usually electrically detonated and weighing about two pounds. Major S's 'claymore' was made out of a very heavy steel plough disc packed with plastic explosive on the concave side and fitted with a detonator in the middle of the explosive. The idea was to face the convex side towards the enemy and detonate it electrically when there was a juicy target in front of it. It was a great idea but then, he didn't have to carry it. It was massively heavy and awkward to carry.

The group comprised Major S as the leader, me as the radio operator, some regular soldiers and the rest Territorial Force (TF). There was only a minimal briefing and no pre-op training, such as practising obstacles, test-firing weapons, practising RV drills and man-down drills. This was another Scouts' 'off-the-cuff' operation.

We helicoptered in to Mozambique in five helicopters at last light. After trying to walk noiselessly, we gave up. The claymore was carried on a pole by two men but it kept swaying from side to side and was problematic to control, not to mention exhausting. Frequently changing carriers was necessary and time-consuming and the going was difficult. The ground was very soft sand and the vegetation was thick which meant one could not walk in a straight line: one had to walk around the clumps of thick bush. The ten-kilometre march to the target turned out to be much longer.

On reaching the target, the road was recce'd and it was decided we should move our position to one better suited to ambush. We moved back into the bush and proceeded north as it started to rain. That night we moved into a laying-up position well away from the road. I set up my Australian bivvie sheet and made sure it was going to keep the water off me. Light drizzle turned into a heavy downpour that went on for hours. I took the opportunity to collect water off my bivvie and before long, all my bottles were full. When dawn arrived the rain had stopped. I was dry and had had a good sleep but several others were saturated. Their morale was low.

Rich and Rory had a lot of kit captured from terrorists, such as Brit webbing and German mess kits. The German mess kits were appalling. The mugs were small and the mess tins were a peculiar shape and useless. I always carried three mugs, one for a brew, one for rice and one for curry. They begged me to give them one mug each because their stupid little mugs were useless. I had one of my feelings of something about to go wrong. I could vividly see in my mind's eye my mugs getting lost. I said, "You are going to lose my mugs."

"Oh no we won't!" they insisted and so against my better judgement I gave them one mug between them. Better to lose one mug than two.

Major S came along with the message for the morning radio schedule. I set up the radio antenna and encoded the message then sent it off in Morse code, including our location and a situation report.

And then a dog found us. This was bad news. Where there are dogs there are people. We hurriedly packed up and moved off. As you can imagine, after all that rain our feet sank into the soft sand and we left a trail a blind man could follow. We walked all day and followed a bearing to take us to the road which we hit at mid-afternoon. At 1800 hours Major S gave me the message for the evening radio schedule. I got it encoded and established communications with base using Morse code. I was about halfway through sending the message when I heard *pop, pop, pop, pop* and screams of pain coming from the direction of the route we had come in on. Major S rushed up and said, "Those are the anti-personnel mines I put down. It's the Freds [Frelimo]." I stopped sending immediately and packed up the radio kit. Incoming automatic fire began ripping the bush over my head. Several Frelimo troops had lost feet or legs so they were angry. The Portuguese anti-personnel mines were small and very effective. We all got into a single file and followed the major. The world's largest claymore is probably still where we left it.

We moved off towards the Cabora Bassa power lines which travel parallel with the Rhodesian border about twenty kilometres inside Mozambique. Once we hit the power lines, the idea was to call for helicopter uplift. Why did we not carry on with mission? I simply don't know because it was never explained to me.

We were watching the road running alongside the power lines from behind an earth bank when we spotted a group of Frelimo soldiers in single file about 300 metres away. They were walking tactically and clearly expecting trouble. As they approached we gave them a rip from our rifles. They replied immediately and charged. They were good. I have a vivid impression of firing at the Frelimo and out of the corner of my eye I could see Rich and Rory discarding their rucksacks and running away. I turned to get a better look and could see I was the only one left. My colleagues had deserted me! There was abandoned equipment lying on the ground and Frelimo were coming to get me.

Keeping all my kit with me, I followed the spoor of my fleeing colleagues. I couldn't keep up. I had a full rucksack on my back, with high-frequency radio, spare batteries and all the rest of my gear and the guys in front were carrying nothing, relatively speaking. After an hour at full speed in a generally easterly direction, I had to stop for a rest. I did a dogleg and watched my own spoor to see if I was being followed. The ground here was sloping gently downhill which meant I was on the edge of the escarpment which led down to the Nuanetsi river. The vegetation was beginning to thin out. It was mid-afternoon by now and would be dark in a few hours.

And then I heard the sound of helicopters to the south. By climbing a small tree I could see them. They were only a kilometre away and were circling. I did not have a small VHF voice radio, so I erected the high-frequency radio and used a whip antenna about six feet long. When I switched on I could hear a chopper calling me. Oh joy! After a short while, a chopper came over to my location but there was nowhere to land due to the vegetation so the pilot sat the Alouette III on top of a large bush. I handed my rucksack up to the tech/gunner and he pulled me up. The tech was 'Flash' Gordon who was later killed on a Fire Force contact when he stopped a bullet.

On returning to the fort at Chiredzi, the pilot put me down right in the middle of the fort. Good bloke. Everyone else was back by that time. Squadron Leader Fenton-Wells, the air liaison officer at the fort and known as 'Frantan' after the locally made napalm, was glad to see me. He said, "I knew there was something wrong as soon as you cut your radio transmission in mid-stride. So I scrambled some blues from here to see what the problem was." That man knew what he was doing and it was lucky he was there at that time; without him there could have been a major problem.

Major S, however, said something to the effect of, "So, you're back then?" and that was all. There was no debrief, no analysis of events and no lessons learned. It was a totally unprofessional end to an unprofessional operation.

After The Operation That Went Wrong and now this cock-up, I wanted to get away from unprofessional people and out of this sort of outfit, quickly. I had had enough. I joined 6 Troop, a pseudo troop, a few days later which was led by a mature, long-service senior NCO called Pete MacNeilage. Things got immeasurably better. I had had enough of going on jobs organized by people who did not have a clue. By comparison, Pete knew how to give briefings and debriefings and although quick to discipline he knew when and how to motivate. He was a refreshing change.

How I joined the Selous Scouts and met my wife
Or how the Selous Scouts (and a few others) found me a wife!

My wife and I celebrated our thirty-second wedding anniversary recently which set me thinking about how our marriage was so entwined with the Scouts and everything that led on from those days. How can that be, you might ask?

I served with the Artists Rifles, B Squadron 21 SAS from 1968 to 1972. Those were sunny days when life was good. The training was excellent and I made lots of good friends, which I still see to this day. But it's a funny thing that the more training and exercises you do, the more you want the real thing. And that's the way it was with me.

I joined the Rhodesian army in 1974, passed selection for SAS straight away and was posted into A Troop. This troop was the Regular Troop, which had a large number of enlisted foreign soldiers. B Troop was mainly territorial soldiers with some Rhodesian regulars. Those days too were sunny days and life was good. A Troop got its share of the action in what must have been one of the final African colonial wars. Life was hectic with operational jumps, armoured columns, combat tracking, sabotage, camp attacks, near misses and some not-so-near misses. I served alongside Americans, French, Portuguese, New Zealanders, Australians, a Pole, a German, South Africans, a Canadian and a few more besides. But it's a funny thing that the more action you get, the more you want. And that's the way it was with me.

By 1976, the Selous Scouts had been in existence for two years and were making a name for themselves in the counter-insurgency role. What would it be like, I thought, to work alongside turned terrorists hunting and tracking their former comrades? After passing the Scouts selection course, which is a story in itself, and then the Dark Phase where I learned to be a terrorist, I was posted to 6 Troop. What a shock I had when I met those guys for the first time on the day we deployed to our area of operations. Out of the troop barrack room emerged a rag-tag bunch of blacks, dressed mostly in blue denim, long hair tied in spikey lumps, with pistols stuck in belts, AK rifles or RPD machine guns over their shoulders, the guy with his battery-powered record player on his head (playing a record – always!), others with transistor radios or chewing on doorsteps of bread. These were the men that the other white soldier and I were going to be living cheek by jowl with for the next four to six weeks. This was a culture shock for a boy from West London.

However, after a couple of bush trips I got used to it. Deploying to an area, establishing a bush camp and being briefed with specific intelligence for an operation by Special Branch became normal routine.

In mid-1977, 6 Troop was settled into a bush camp near Lake Kyle outside Fort Victoria. The troop commander, Pete, and I set off dressed in our denim jeans and in our civilian Mercedes 2.5-ton truck for our meeting with SB at a very special rendezvous. The special RV in fact was the Zimbabwe Ruins hotel where we hoped that, with a bit of luck, SB would pay for some of the refreshments we would consume during the briefing. On the way to the hotel we passed the Zimbabwe Ruins, a collection of ancient dry-stone-walled buildings constructed some 900 years ago. It was a dry and dusty day and the sun was strong enough to burn your eyeballs out. Walking along the road in the direction of the hotel were four whites, two men and two girls. Racing past them in our truck we covered them in a cloud of dust.

"Stop and give them a lift," said Pete.

"No, can't stop," I replied. We'll be late for the pub."

Well, the boss is the boss, so we stopped. Orders are orders. I unhooked the tailgate and helped the civvies into the rear of the wagon. One of the guys looked familiar. At the hotel the civvies treated us to a couple of drinks which made it all worthwhile. SB was late as usual. Over a few more drinks it suddenly 'clicked.' The familiar face was Roger 'Eddie' Edmonds, ex Artists Rifles, A Squadron 21 SAS who later went off to join R Squadron 22 SAS, based at Hereford. Of course, this led to a few more drinks, and then a few more. As the sun began to disappear, so did Roger. Suddenly I was alone with Miss Holliday. Now, would I chat up another guy's chick? Would I get her phone number even if she was friendly with someone I knew? You're damned right I would.

Three years later we were married and thirty-two years, three children and a grandchild later, I'm sitting here saying, "That's the way it was." Cheers Roger! (Roger still speaks to me and all is well on the home front!!)

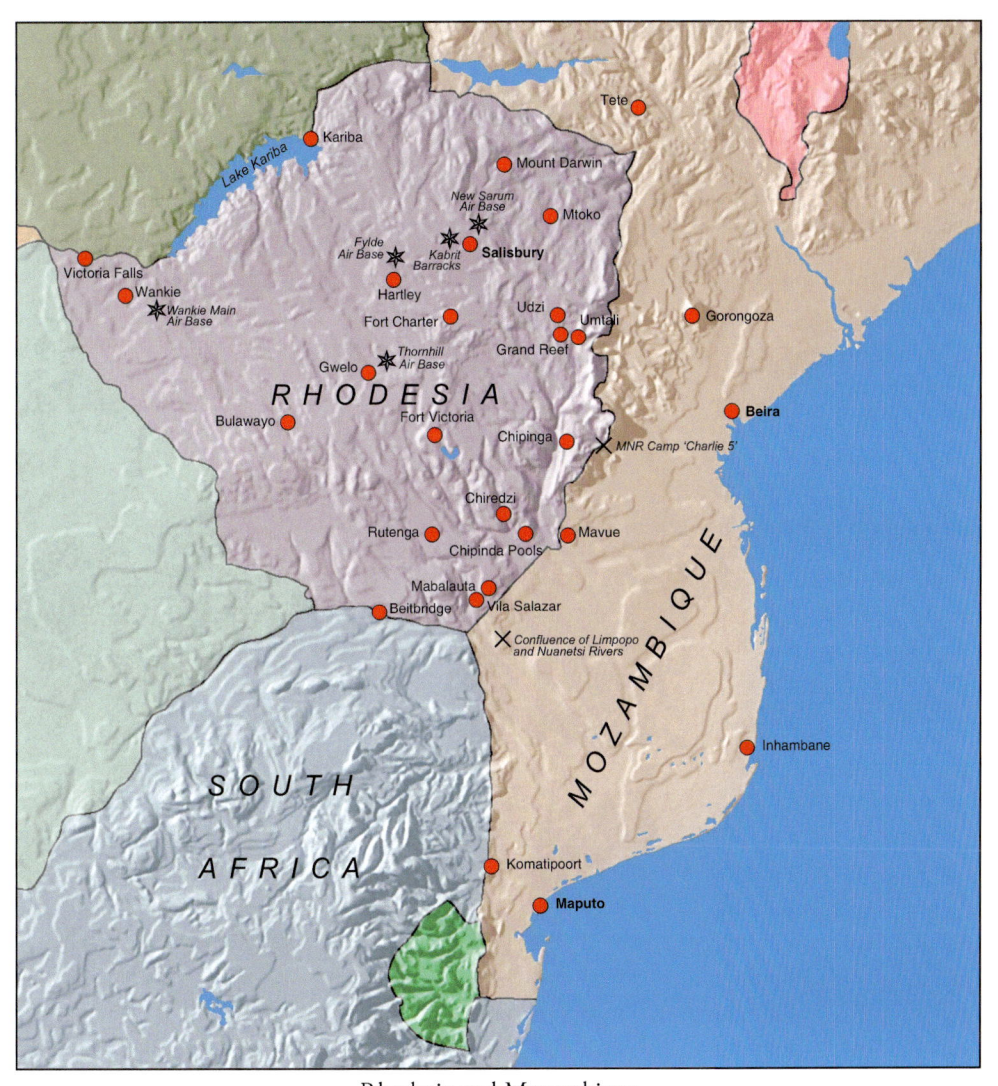

Rhodesia and Mozambique

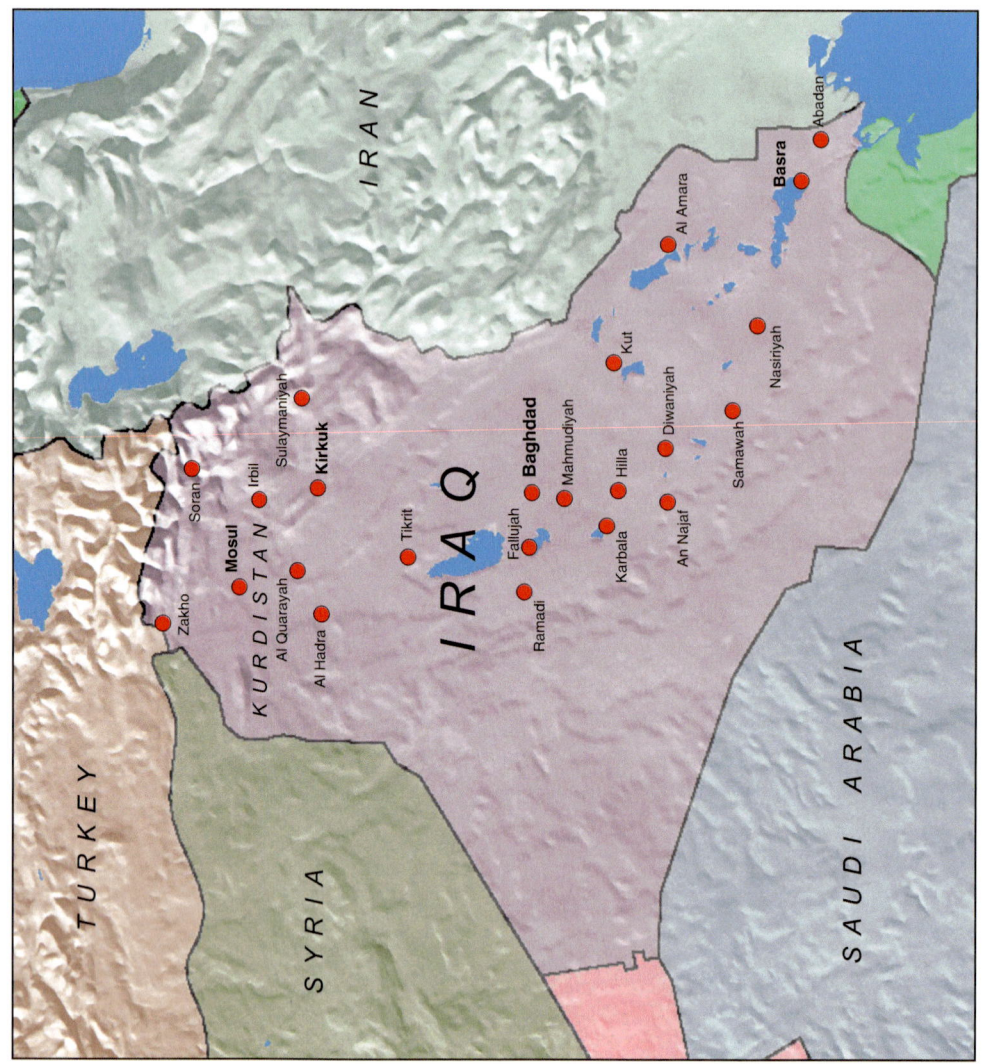

Iraq and Kurdistan

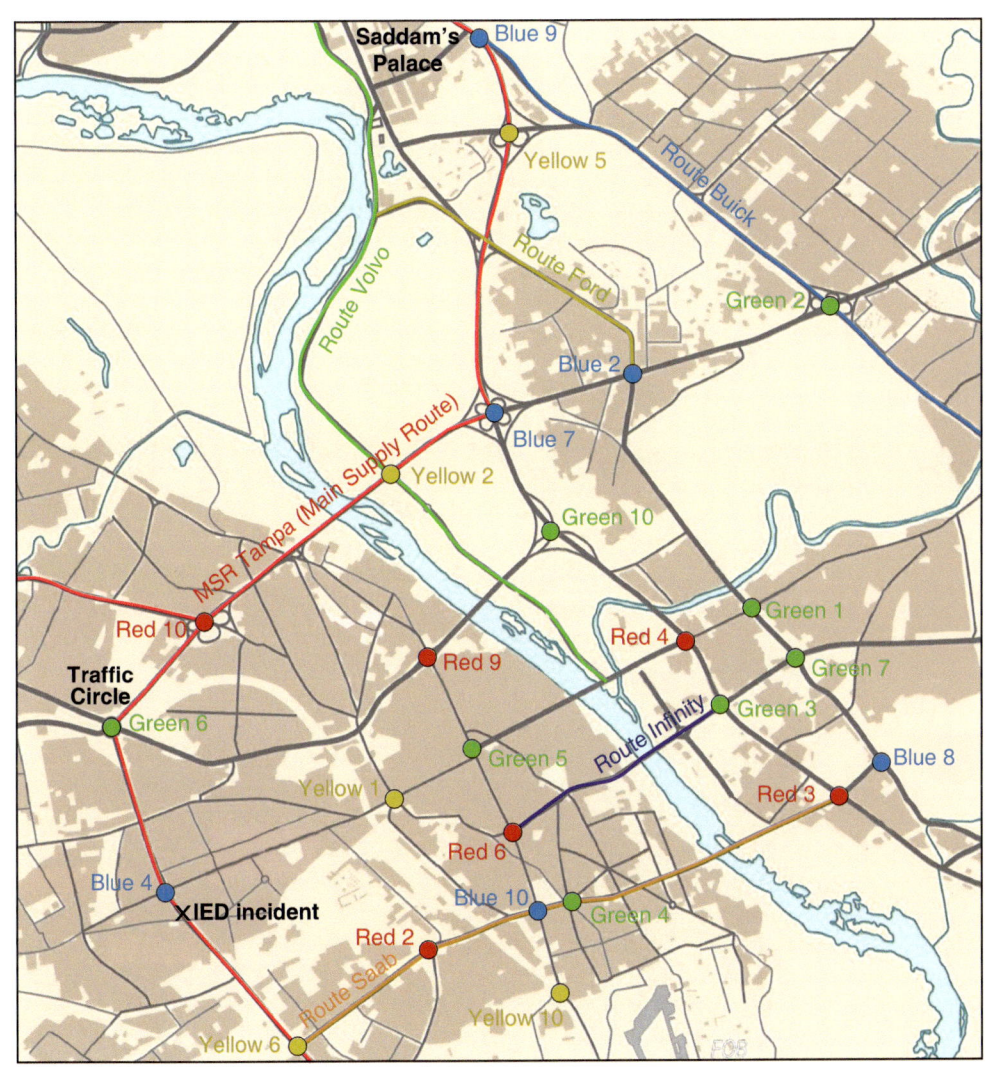

Mosul City, Iraq

Rhodesian National Parachute Championships, 1975. Back from left: Boss Douglas (RhAF), Kevin Milligan (RhAF), Paul Hogan (RhAF), J.C. Grey (SAS), Mike Wiltshire (RhAF). Front from left: J. Hurly (RhAF), J. Lang (SAS) and the author.

Author's Rhodesian SAS Parachute Log book.

SAS Log Book entry: Operational Jump – 15/01/79 – static line into Zambia

SAS Log Book entries: Operational Jump – 09/06/79 – static line into Mozambique; Operational Jump – 07/07/79 – static line into Mozambique; Operational Jump – 4/10/79 – Freefall into Zambia – Operation Cheese

Author's Selous Scout Parachute logbook

Selous Scouts Log Book entry: Operational Jump – 24/10/76 – freefall into Mozambique

6 Troop Selous Scouts in a base camp preparing dinner.

Cpl Frank Ephraim of 6 Troop Selous Scouts walking off the drop zone.

6 Troop Selous Scouts para-trained element, 1977. The author is sixth from left.

1978, the new Bell Huey helicopters at New Sarum. The author is second from right.

Cleaning a 76mm recoilless rifle.

Raid on Joshua Nkomo 1979 – the ferry *Sea Lion* in transit on Lake Kariba.

Raid on Joshua Nkomo 1979 – Land Rovers on board the *Sea Lion*.

Raid on Joshua Nkomo 1979 – Andy Anderson standing on rear of Land Rover.

Raid on Joshua Nkomo 1979 – The Land Rover that broke down.

Raid on Joshua Nkomo 1979 – The author's Land Rover. The author is on the front machine gun and Cpl Anton Grobler is standing at back.

Grand Reef airfield, 1979. A call-sign waits for a helicopter before deploying to Mozambique.

A ZANLA camp in Mozambique, 1979. Jimmy Ramsay about to enter a bunker. *Photo* author's collection

Kabrit barracks, 1979. A Huey helicopter returns a call sign after a deployment.

Chipinga, 10 June 1979. C Squadron returned from a road ambush in Mozambique. Author is at extreme right.

Security force patrols during the election in Salisbury, March 1980.

Mr and Mrs French after the wedding, 21 March 1980.

The wedding party. From left: Pete and Trish Leonard, Frank Kaszas,
Di Squairs, the author and Mrs French, Doug Parker.

Rhodesian SAS 106mm recoilless rifles at Inkomo range, 1980.

6 Recce Commando training jump at Duku Duku, Zululand, 1980.

Rear L-R: Rhodesian camo shirt with sergeant's stripes, SAS camo shirt wings, Selous Scout beret, British SAS beret, South African Reconnaissance Commando beret, Rhodesian camo shirt with sergeant's stripes and Scouts camo shirt wings. Centre L-R: Selous Scouts operator's wings, Rhodesian infantry combat badge. Front L-R : British SAS stable belt, medals, Selous Scout stable belt.

50th anniversary of the SAS. Free-fallers, Johannesburg, 1991.

50th anniversary of the SAS. All jumpers and the DC-3, Johannesburg, 1991.

Angolan Air Force Mi8 helicopter with parachute display team, Luanda, 1993.

Angolan Air Force Parachute School, Luanda, 1993. From left: Tenente Francisco and Capitão Diamante.

UN compound, Mogadishu, Somalia, 1994.

Mogadishu from the air, UN compound in foreground.

Author with Nepalese security personnel, Iraq, 2005.

Mosul, 2004, Eugene Pomeroy with repaired vehicle following IED blast.

Call sign 30C, Mosul, Iraq, 2004. Eugene Pomeroy kneeling at left, author kneeling centre.

Author with Fijian security personnel.

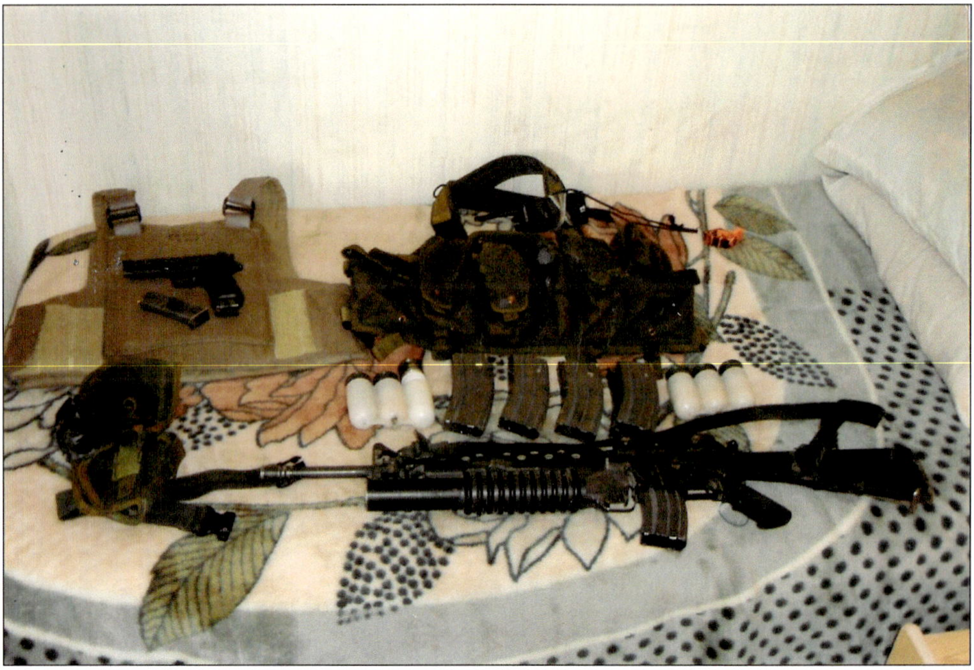

Tools of the trade, Q-West airfield, Iraq 2004/5.

Skydive Dubai, February 2012, the author at extreme left. *Photo* Pete Marsden

How I opened my big mouth and made a career statement

In 1978, towards the end of my service in the Selous Scouts, I was left in charge of the troop for a couple of weeks. We were working in the pseudo role in Chibi Tribal Trust Land. I was with my three bodyguards, Frank E, Simon Chikuponya and Edison, on top of a large domed feature which had a few bushes on one side with a good view of the kraal complex, where our lads had been welcomed by the locals. They were posing as a group infiltrating from Mozambique with resupplies. Good intelligence had been received from the villagers and it was time for the group to move on. We had been deployed for six weeks and I was living on half rations and with a much reduced water supply.

One day I received a radio message from our Selous Scouts fort at Chiredzi instructing me to move the troop to a point for uplift outside the TTL, where they would be picked up by helicopter and flown to the Iron Ore mine which we could see from our feature. It was the open-caste mine which seemed to make the mountain glow almost red in the morning and evening sun. There would be enclosed trucks at the mine waiting to transport us back to Chiredzi.

When my men below came up on the 'small means', the VHF voice radio, that evening I gave them the bad news that they would have to take leave of their girlfriends and make their way to the helicopter pick-up-point the following night. The next night I walked off the feature with my three colleagues and rendezvoused with the troop at a pre-arranged location. We marched off the feature in single file with my three colleagues in front and me at the rear. At dawn the choppers arrived to collect us and take us to the mine.

At the mine we found the trucks waiting with crates of beer in each truck provided by the mine management. Imagine my delight! I was able to rehydrate with Castle Lager! Oh joy of joys! After six weeks on poor food and little water for the last fortnight, I was a slightly inebriated by the time we rolled into the Scouts fort. The fort commander, Major S, met us and told me to go to the ops room for a quick debrief before I went to the Special Branch office with the black NCOs for the SB debrief. I quickly got the black troops into their billet, dumped my kit and went to the ops room, basically a room with walls covered in maps of the area and radios and telephones. In the room were the 5 Troop whites, including my mate Joe Bresler. We shared a laugh and a few jokes while waiting for the major; I was still quite merry. The major entered the room and after a general chat, said to me, "After your handling of the troop these past few weeks, we should think about getting you a commission."

This fazed me; I did not think he was being serious but quick as a flash I replied, "I don't know if I'm stupid enough to be an officer, ha ha, ha."

Well, you could have heard a pin drop. There was total silence as the faux pas dawned on me. Joe's jaw had dropped and he was looking at me as if to say, "You idiot."

After a long pause, the major replied, "And I don't know if I'm clever enough to put you on a charge."

The Demon Drink had struck again and Major S gave me an awful confidential report later on.

How I landed in a tree and lost my hearing

C Squadron was warned off for another operation, named Bouncer, at mid-morning on Friday, 9 June 1979, while we were based at Grand Reef Fire Force base near Umtali in eastern Rhodesia. Operation Bouncer was the name given to an ambush operation based on specific intelligence from Special Branch and activated at very short notice. There must have been dozens of these ops over the years. In this case, intelligence indicated that the target person would be travelling in a Toyota Land Cruiser, escorted by a lorry load of terrorists, on a specific road in Mozambique at a specific time. Time was of the essence and sixteen of us were to emplane that Friday, 9 June, in a DC-3 Dakota, jump into Mozambique and ambush the convoy. The plan was a classic road ambush. A killer group of eight men would lie in the ambush position, two call signs, each of four men, would become the 'end stops', based some distance from the killer group and from where they could watch the road and warn of approaching vehicles. A nominated rocketeer in the killer group, armed with an RPG-7 rocket launcher, would stop the first vehicle and the killer group would then kill everybody in the convoy.

I was in command of one of the end stops. I packed two rifle anti-tank grenades, FN rifle, 600 rounds, grenades, VHF radio, batteries, food and water for five days and the usual sleeping gear. On my body I wore my chest webbing with rifle ammunition and belt webbing with pistol, water, twenty-four hours' food, grenades and survival kit. The rifle grenades were wrapped up in my sleeping bag and groundsheet and would be used to prevent vehicles from approaching the killing ground after the ambush had been initiated. My FN rifle went over my right shoulder and my rucksack was wrapped up in the 'Carrying Straps Personal Equipment Parachutist'. The CSPEP would hook onto my parachute 'D' rings and was also attached to my right leg by a leg strap. In addition to all this, I had my main parachute, reserve parachute and steel helmet. This was a relatively 'light' load because I did not have to carry a high-frequency radio and spare batteries, nor did I have to carry ten days' rations or any explosives. We wore the green Frelimo-type uniforms of shirt and trousers which we always wore on external ops. My stick comprised Brian 'Andy' Anderson (ex-22 SAS) and two Rhodesians. The other end stop on the other side of the killer group also carried two anti-tank rifle grenades.

We emplaned half an hour before dark and immediately headed for Mozambique. The pilot flew extremely low. At one stage I remember looking up at some trees. The principal threat to the aircraft was the hand-held SAM-7 anti-aircraft missile, or Strela, which we knew the terrorists had. They had already shot down two Air Rhodesia Viscount passenger aircraft with them. Aircraft either had to fly below 700 feet above ground level or above 7,000 feet in order to be out of range of these missiles.

We were close to the target in thirty minutes and received the order from the dispatchers to "Stand up, hook up and check equipment!" We would be jumping in one straight stick of sixteen. I took my pistol, a Browning Hi-Power semi-automatic, out of my belt holster and stuck it under the pack opening bands of my belly-mounted reserve parachute. We all did this. On one camp attack a friend of mine had parachuted into a tree and was hanging upside down listening to the automatic fire getting closer. He had his rifle slung over his shoulder, but could not reach it and had difficulty drawing his pistol out of the belt holster. From that time on all personnel on static-line parachute deployments carried a loaded pistol under the elasticated pack opening bands of the reserve parachute.

I remember hooking up and looking out of the window at the trees almost on the same level as the aircraft. The sun was going down and the shadows of the trees were very long. The scene outside was peaceful. We were given the order "Move to the door" and all of us in the port stick shuffled forward so that the number one in the stick was one step back from the door. The aircraft was bouncing around at this stage in some turbulence.

Suddenly the plane made a ninety-degree left turn and we flew over a tar road. This was the target. Then the aircraft made another ninety-degree left turn and the aeroplane climbed like a lift. The G force was considerable and made the kit strapped to me feel as if it weighed twice as much. It did not last long as the plane levelled off and we got the green light to "Go!" We were out of the plane in quick time and I remember looking around me. The canopy oscillated twice and I saw a tree coming towards me. I went into the tree. It was about fifty feet high. I guess we had jumped from 200, maybe 250 feet. I wasn't in the air and under canopy for more than fifteen seconds. As I was hanging in the tree, I remember thinking we were far too close to the road and that I wished I had a steerable canopy instead of the standard unsteerable type. If my canopy had been steerable, and steerable canopies were available, I might have landed next to the tree instead of on top of it. This was an operational descent and there was a risk the canopies would not return to Rhodesia, so consequently we had been issued the old unsteerable parachutes.

I was about half way up the tree and almost upside down. My left leg was in one of the rigging lines and the rucksack was still on my right leg. While I was under canopy I had made the decision not to release the CSPEP on the fifteen-foot suspension rope in case it caught in the tree I was drifting towards and swung me into the ground. As I kicked my left leg out of the suspension lines the canopy came unhooked from the tree. I fell about fifteen feet until the canopy again got caught in the branches. I was now about ten feet off the ground. I jettisoned the CSPEP and the rucksack bounced off a rock on the ground. I pulled the reserve parachute and after unhooking one side, I climbed down the lines. I got my FN off my shoulder and cocked the weapon. I unwrapped my rucksack from the CSPEP. First fight and then survive.

Getting the canopy out of the tree was a sod of a job and I had to cut some lines to achieve this. 'They' were always warning us not to cut lines but 'they' worked in offices. Putting my rucksack on my back, with my main and reserve canopies on top and my rifle in my hand, I set off for the rendezvous point in the centre of the line of parachutists where all the parachuting kit would be stored.

Once everybody had made their way to the rendezvous, we shook out into formation and set off for the road. It did not take long to get there as we had been dropped far too close to target. An ambush position was selected for the ambush party. Unfortunately, we did not know from which direction the vehicles would approach. From the selected ambush position vehicles could be ambushed from either direction. I took my stop group up the road for about 1,500 metres and selected a good place from which to watch the road and set up my VHF radio with a remote 'sputnik' antenna up a convenient tree. However, we had bad VHF communications with the ambush group and had to relocate. We had to move closer to the ambush group which was unavoidable due to the nature of the ground and the necessity for good communications. We settled down for what we thought might be a wait of several days. That night we slept in a line and each person stood guard for two hours.

Morning arrived but no convoy. I fitted one of my rifle grenades, a South African 28R, to my FN rifle and put the 'ballastite' cartridge, a sort of blank round, into the breech of the rifle. If by accident one used a real bullet on a 28R, one would not live to tell the tale. One had to be very careful. We were ready for anything. I had the FN ready with an anti-tank grenade and my 'buddy' Link had an RPD belt-fed machine gun. Andy also had an FN rifle and his 'buddy' an RPD. For just four men, that gave us a lot of firepower.

As soon as it was daylight two men moved back from the road about ten metres into a sheltered spot and had a feed and a brew. When they returned to the ambush position the other two went off and had their feed. Our rucksacks were always packed and ready to move at a moment's notice.

At exactly 1700 hours that day, Saturday, 10 June, the convoy arrived from the other direction. Initially there was a loud bang, the RPG-7 I guess, fired by Jannie, and then there was an intense amount of automatic fire. From our left, around a bend in the road, came a single Mercedes truck. My 3 colleagues pumped automatic fire into it and I got ready to put a rifle grenade into it. I put the FN into my shoulder and leaned into the weapon. I moved forward and took aim along the top of the grenade and slowly squeezed the trigger. Firing an anti-tank grenade in the 'approved' manner from the hip is very inaccurate. I preferred shooting a rifle grenade from the shoulder. I fired and suddenly everything went white and quiet. I thought I was dead. There was total silence, there was a white mist. I thought to myself, "So this is what it's like to be dead." The mist cleared and I saw the end of my rifle. I touched the end of my rifle. This proved I wasn't dead.

Turning around, I saw my three colleagues on the ground. "Get up, you silly buggers," I said." Andy said something but I couldn't hear.

The truck had stopped on the left of the road with the front left wheel in a ditch. The driver jumped down. He was the only person in the vehicle. He started to run. Link got him. The sounds of battle from up the road had stopped, so we picked up our rucksacks and set off to rejoin the main ambush party. I moved over to the truck and pumped some rounds into the fuel tank on the right-hand side. Fuel poured out. When we were a safe distance from the truck I threw a white phosphorus grenade under the vehicle. That should have set it well alight. It didn't. It wasn't diesel in the tank, probably sunflower oil or old engine oil or something similar.

We hooked up with our colleagues in the killer group who were busy counting bodies. They counted sixty-five. All the vehicles were burning, the truck was on its side and there were bodies everywhere. With the bodies, flames, smoke and the wrecked vehicles, it was better than the movie *Apocalypse Now*.

When everybody was together a head count was made and the column set off for the parachute cache, where the signaller sent a situation report requesting uplift next morning. Later that night several vehicles were heard to arrive at the contact scene and bursts of automatic fire were heard but they declined to come looking for us.

Two Bell Huey helicopters arrived at first light and we returned to Grand Reef before flying back to Salisbury. Everything was fine except that I was completely deaf for months.

The problem with the 28R rifle grenade, I believe, was the arming mechanism. The grenade is normally 'safe' when fired and arms after twenty metres when the inertia, or reaction to the force of being fired, moves a metal sleeve back over a tube. This movement allows the weapon to become armed. I think that dropping it out of the tree armed the weapon by moving the sleeve over the tube, so when I fired the grenade the firing pin moved forward and there was no sleeve in place to block this movement. Consequently, the grenade detonated about twenty feet from the end of my rifle.

6

Raid on Joshua Nkomo, Lusaka, 14 April 1979

About seven days before this raid was due to take place, C Squadron was on morning muster parade at Kabrit barracks and was given a warning order that an operation was imminent. The Squadron Commander, Captain Martin 'Percy' Pearce, issued lists of equipment to various NCOs to be drawn from the QM, MT and ammo stores and loaded onto the squadron vehicles. My task was to draw ammunition and pyrotechnics and load them onto the ammo truck. Other NCOs drew vehicle paint, brushes, jerry cans, tentage and so on. In addition, seven old Sabre Land Rovers were drawn from MT; they were petrol-driven and long wheelbase, leftovers from the border-control days of the 1960s. They were used for driver training and as runabouts and had not been on ops for years. It was obvious now that the op was to be vehicle-borne and would be a moderately deep external raid into a neighbouring country.

Interestingly, we were ordered to pack only Rhodesian camouflage clothing and to take both AK rifles and webbing as well as FN rifles. The SAS 2 i/c, Grahame Wilson, would be coming along as operational commander. Bringing in this 'outsider' caused some consternation among the rank and file: we knew we could do the job on our own. Vehicles were allocated and it was clear the op would comprise the seven Sabres, each with five men on board. Each vehicle had one forward-firing MAG belt-fed machine gun and one post-mounted MAG at the rear.

Selection of personnel was made by Captain Pearce and Lieutenant Cook. The unlucky members of the squadron would remain behind at the advanced base as rear party to guard the camp.

There were two officers, the Rhodesian Pearce and Cook from New Zealand, as well as several sergeants. Others included Andy Anderson, a Brit ex-22 SAS man. C Squadron was low on foreigners compared to other squadrons and was mostly Rhodesian. A Squadron, for instance, was high on foreigners and included Canadian, German, Aussie, American and others.

The morning following the Warning Order, C Squadron left Kabrit in convoy and headed to an unknown security-sterile location to train for the operation. The convoy comprised the seven Sabres, an ammo truck, stores truck, kitchen truck, MT truck and I think a Pig armoured car. We had one vehicle mechanic with us, Bunny Hardt, whom I had known in the Selous Scouts. We headed north to Sinoia where we picked up his cousin, another vehicle mechanic, and continued north to Kariba airfield. At Kariba a tent camp was established near the airfield, well away from prying eyes. After a preliminary briefing where the target was disclosed, a model and photos were then used as training aids. In addition, an area the approximate size of the target house was marked out and roped off to provide an idea of the size of the target area.

Joshua Nkomo, leader of ZAPU was the target.

It was known that Nkomo rarely slept two nights at the same house. Specific intelligence had been received, indicating that he would be at a particular house in a Lusaka suburb on the night of 14 April. The house had been photographed by a spy living in Lusaka, but the photos were of poor quality and showed little except that the house was a single-storey structure typical of middle-class suburbs in Africa, and was on a plot a third of an acre size with a five-foot-high wire fence all round.

We were to use a Kariba car ferry, the *Sea Lion*, operated by the Rhodesian Engineers, to cross the lake, and would have high-level air cover all the way to the Zambian shore. An SAS patrol was at that time in Zambia undertaking a recce of the landing point. Once ashore, we would form into a line of march and then make directly for Lusaka.

At the target area, one Land Rover crew would form a roadblock while the house was assaulted. All Nkomo's guards in the garden were to be removed from the game using the belt-fed MAG machine guns mounted on the Land Rovers. The house would then be turned into rubble using bunker bombs; made from lengths of plastic pipe about four inches in diameter, filled with plastic explosive and fitted with hand-grenade detonators. These were amazingly effective at destroying buildings. Once the building was rubble, house-clearing teams would enter the ruins and search for Nkomo. Exfiltration would be carried out on the same route that we used on the way in. Using the same route both in and out is bad practice but was unavoidable due to the lack of roads in the area. The main danger points for us would be crossing the Kafue river bridge, guarded by Zambian army troops, and the exfiltration phase from

Lusaka.

No one questioned the feasibility of the operation, since we all had no doubt we could pull it off. Our security at Kariba was total. Nobody came into the camp or went out except the OC, Captain Pearce. As far as anyone was concerned, we were there for training. This was a security-sterile environment.

The night before we were due to embark on the ferry, the Land Rovers were hand-painted in approximate Zambian camouflage by Bunny and his cousin. The following morning, before dawn, we embarked on the ferry and set off across the lake. Bunny and his cousin did not come with us. No vehicle repair tools were carried, so if a vehicle broke down it was to be destroyed if beyond local repair. We had a job getting all seven Sabres on the ferry but somehow we manhandled them on and squeezed them in. On board we met the two Selous Scouts who were to accompany us. The Scouts lieutenant, White, whom I knew, had travelled the route before. With him was a black soldier, Aaron, whom I had served with in 6 Troop. He had been the troop sergeant until he was reduced to the ranks and dispatched to the Scouts' guard force for womanizing, when he should have been operating, and for lying about it to Pete, the Troop commander. He had clearly been rehabilitated and was now working in Scouts Recce Troop. White and Aaron would be in the lead vehicle and Aaron was to talk our way through any roadblocks we might come across.

The *Sea Lion* ferry arrived at the landing point on time. We made communications with the call sign on the shore waiting for us, led by Sergeant Wilhelm Ratte. Wilhelm had chosen a first-class landing area and it was easy to drive ashore. After disembarking, we formed into the line of march and set off immediately as night was falling. The *Sea Lion* was then parked up under some overhanging trees on the shore to await our return.

The track we were to use to access the Great North Road was a poor quality dirt track with ruts and potholes and had seen little use recently. With the moonlight it made for easy driving. The region was a mix of flat, wet *vleis*, or marshes, and lightly wooded areas.

Our call sign comprised Lieutenant Cook, me on the front MAG, the driver Oranges, Billy and Sean on the rear post-mounted MAG. Time was of the essence and we drove as fast as we could. One area was particularly wet and after hitting a deep pothole with a bone-shattering jolt, our Land Rover was covered in water. Then the engine cut out. Wilson gave us fifteen minutes to get the engine started or we would be left behind. The vehicle was pushed under some trees and we went to work on the engine. All the water was cleaned off and the electrical connections checked and dried. Oranges tried the starter but the motor wouldn't fire. Wilson gave us the bad news that we would be left behind and collected on the way back. This was the right decision in the circumstances. Leaving us behind deprived the operation of considerable firepower but the exfiltration from Lusaka needed to be completed in darkness and fixing our Land Rover would waste valuable time. Later some argued that we should have taken Bunny Hardt the mechanic with us. However, the decision not to include him had long been made and it was now too late. The convoy left immediately. We dismounted the belt-fed MAGs and went into the bush. That night we took it in turns to each do one hour of sentry while the rest slept.

The convoy made it to the main Lusaka road and bluffed their way through the checkpoint at the Kafue river bridge, with Aaron screaming at the guard who nervously waved them through. Once in Lusaka, they arrived at Nkomo's house. The plan worked perfectly. The guards in the garden were all killed and the building was bunker-bombed to rubble. But sadly, Nkomo was not at home.

The assault group completed the mission with only one casualty, Barry Derry, who took a round in his bum but luckily he received no lasting damage and was back in action later that year. The bullet had missed his hip joint by an inch. Sadly, Pearce was killed on another operation to get Nkomo a short time later.

Next day, at about midday, much later than was planned, we heard the convoy calling us on the 'small means' VHF radio. When the convoy arrived we hooked up our dead Land Rover to Andy Anderson's vehicle and set off homeward bound. After a while Oranges our driver put the vehicle in gear and switched on the ignition. When he let out the clutch, amazingly the engine started. We stopped to untie the tow rope and continued under our own power. However, the convoy stopped again after only a few minutes. The vehicle behind us had broken down. It had hit a massive hole and a tie-bar, part of the steering mechanism, had broken. Time was getting on and Wilson made the decision to destroy the vehicle. The Land Rover was stripped out quickly and then burned. The crew jumped on other vehicles and after a quick head-count we set off to the landing point.

The return was completely uneventful. After embarking on the Sea Lion, which was much easier than it had been previously since we were one vehicle less, we slept most of the way to Kariba. After packing up our camp and enjoying a good shower we drove to Sinoia where we dropped off Bunny's cousin. Then we headed for Salisbury and home.

7
The operation that went right

Jack Malloch, when I met him, wasn't young any more. He was overweight and seemed slow to move, but he exuded a calm confidence born of experience, risk-taking and success. He told me he was one of the Rhodesians who had volunteered for flying training in the Second World War, which meant that he was around sixty or slightly older when he dropped me and three others on a free-fall operation in 1979. He was a motivated man who appeared to be accustomed to getting his own way. Jack told me he had been shot down in the south of France during the war and was saved by his parachute. After the war he and a friend, bought a surplus DC-3 Dakota transport aeroplane using their end-of-service gratuities and "made lots of money" during the 1948/49 Berlin Airlift. They then bought another DC-3 and formed Air Trans Africa. During the Nigerian civil war of 1967–69, when Biafra, the southwestern oil-rich province declared independence, ATA was heavily involved in flying supplies to the rebels. It seems Jack became too heavily involved and when the airfield at the town of Warri, in the southeast of Nigeria, was overrun he lost everything. That didn't stop him. He was bank-rolled by the Rhodesian government and ATA was back in business, beating the sanctions that had been applied by the UN and successive British governments. Among other products, he was air-freighting Rhodesian beef wrapped in plastic and labelled 'Produce of Argentina'. By 1979 his fleet comprised mainly four-engined DC-10 jet transports but he still retained a piston-engined DC-7.

Sadly Jack died when the restored Mk21 Spitfire he was flying crashed shortly after the Rhodesian war ended. Jack had done a deal with the Rhodesian Air Force and was given the Spitfire 'Gate Guard' at New Sarum Air Force Base in Salisbury, refurbishing it to almost new condition complete with four 20mm cannon. He was that kind of man. His favourite aeroplane, the DC-7, was a large transport aircraft with four radial piston engines. Sadly, even though Jack called the motors "the finest piston engines ever made", they dropped a lot of oil. The authorities at Salisbury Main made him park the DC-7 far away from other aeroplanes, with a half an oil drum under each engine to catch the leaks. Since it was powered by petrol engines and no longer

THE OPERATION THAT WENT RIGHT

economical to use on international routes, it was hired out to the Rhodesian Air Force for operations and troop transporting. Although it was fitted out as an insulated transport for meat, it could hold sixty men with equipment when trooping. When used for parachuting it could hold forty men with some room to spare. Only Jack would pilot the aeroplane; it was his 'baby'!

My parachute log book tells me that at 0730 hours we did 'a heavy drop attempt' on 29 May 1979 at Darwendale dam, near Salisbury, from the DC-7. I did a static line jump as number six in a stick of twenty. The DC-7 had all the cargo doors removed, which produced a door around eight feet wide. In the aircraft was a wooden ramp which protruded into the slipstream. Loaded on it, the ramp had a wooden pallet about eight feet long x four feet wide x four feet high. On the first run-in the dispatchers, who included our own OC, attempted to push the pallet down the ramp. Unfortunately, the pallet caught the slipstream and jammed sideways in the door which produced a moment of panic before it was man-handled back into the aircraft. Another good idea bit the dust. After clearing the ramp and pallet away, the static-liners were stood up and dispatched into wind conditions which were well 'over the top'. I had previously seen the Motor Transport section at Selous Scouts playing around with a beach-buggy type car that they had cut into two parts to make it suitable for dropping by parachute. I guessed that the 'heavy drop attempt' was the product of someone in the SAS thinking on the same lines. If only SAS and Scouts had cooperated, then duplication of effort might have been avoided. Due to a lack of suitable aircraft the Rhodesian forces could not drop by parachute any load bigger than 200 kilograms.

Towards the end of September 1979, C Squadron was in camp at Kabrit barracks as the Lancaster House conference was under way in London, where the British government had all the sides in the Rhodesian conflict around the negotiating table. The Rhodesians were becoming fed up with the antics of the 'freedom fighters' at the conference, and to propel them into a situation where they would become more compliant, Operation Cheese was given the go-ahead. This was an operation that had been in planning for a year or more.

By destroying strategic bridges in Zambia, the Zambian government would be forced to export and import through Rhodesia. At this time copper was the principal Zambian export and virtually the sole source of foreign currency, with the Zambians reliant to a high degree on imports of maize and fertilizer. The SAS was tasked with dropping the road and rail bridges over the

Chambeshi bridges from Canberra photo recon. *Photo* RhAF

Chambeshi river, a little way south of the Zambian border with Tanzania.

On 25 September, we were given a warning order, a sort of preliminary order with no great detail, and told that we were to be tasked with preparation of kit and four or five training parachute jumps, before moving out of camp to a 'security-sterile' area —on or around 28 October—and that the operation would be launched shortly thereafter. Lance-Corporal Standish-White and I were given an air photo, taken by a Canberra jet bomber, of two bridges spanning a fairly large river and told to make a scale model. Using cardboard, scissors, glue and a ruler we knocked up a fairly realistic model, about four feet square, of the two bridges: one concrete road bridge and one steel rail bridge across a river nearly 200 yards wide. While Standish-White and I were employed on the model, the rest of the squadron were drawing ammunition, plastic explosives, masking tape, plastic bags, rolls of cordtex (a plastic explosive fuse that looks like washing line), detonators, canoes, inflatable boat, radios, batteries and all the other kit one needs for a demolition task of this kind.

We completed two training jumps on 26 September and two more the next day, all from DC-3 Dakota aircraft. On the afternoon of the 27th, sixteen operators, with drivers and storemen, rolled out of camp in our convoy of stores trucks, Land Rovers and armoured personnel carriers to our secret training area. We arrived at a farm near Darwendale dam, about thirty kilometres west of Salisbury, where we set up camp. In this security-sterile environment, no one was allowed out and no one was allowed in, except the SAS Adjutant, who visited every day with the mail, orders and new air photos. A briefing room was set up in one of the rooms in the farmhouse where we installed the model. We finally learned where the targets were located. There was a hush when the pointer went to the top of the map of Zambia, not far from the Tanzanian border. Nobody had ever operated that far away before. It was around 750 kilometres from Salisbury, which was a long walk home if it all turned sour. There were no maps of this area, so we were issued escape maps photocopied from a Zambian Tourist Board map showing 'important' things like petrol stations, tourist rest camps and tourist destinations. I still have mine and I see where I marked distances between towns, secondary roads, and two national parks, North and South Luangwa. Apart from no maps, there was no hope of casevac (casualty evacuation) until the end of the operation. Still, if you can't take a joke don't join the army!

The operation was to be in four phases:

In Phase One, four free-fallers—Major Wilson, Lieutenant Cook, Lance-Corporal Standish-White and myself as signaller—with light kit and 2 canoes, would enter Zambia around fifty kilometres from target and carry out a 'close-in recce'. In this case the recce involved getting up close to the target, ensuring that the target conformed to the dimensions we had estimated off the air photos, and then getting away unseen. The term 'light kit' was a bit of a joke since we would all be carrying ten days' rations, five days' water, radios, batteries, AK rifles, ammunition, grenades, chest webbing and belt order containing emergency rations and kit. Following the close-in recce we would then find a drop zone and await the rest of the team.

In Phase Two, twelve troops with heavy kit, identical to the 'light kit', would enter by static-line parachute. They would bring with them six two-man folding Klepper canoes, one Zodiac inflatable boat with silenced outboard motor, prepared demolition charges and a resupply of rations for the free-fallers. We would then all paddle to the target.

In Phase Three, we would demolish the bridges.

In Phase Four, we would make our exfiltration by hijacking a truck, driving south to a national park, call in Bell ('Huey') helicopters and fly home. Dead easy! It was pointed out that there was no casevac facility available for any of the operators if injured during the operation; it would only be available after completion of the operation.

The next few days involved canoeing on Darwendale dam and testing the inflatable Zodiac boat using realistic weights. On the dam was a ruined house that had been partially submerged when the dam was completed some years before, with only the walls rising above water level. The remains of the house were used for demolition practice. Many hours were spent flogging up and down the dam until we were all pretty well fed up with folding canoes. In addition, we spent hours making up cutting charges of plastic explosive for slicing through the steelwork of the rail bridge and fifty-kilogram boxes of plastic explosive for demolishing the concrete piers of the road bridge. Cordtex 'nets' were prepared for use on the road bridge piers. These nets of cordtex, looking like fishing nets with a 100mm mesh, were to be suspended on the opposite side of the piers from the fifty-kilogram charges and would be detonated 0.05 of a second before the main charge using a cordtex-delay device. The shock wave from the cordtex nets would create a negative pressure on one side of the pier, making it easier for the main charge, tamped by the water above, behind and below, and detonated 0.05 of a second later, to demolish the pier.

On the night of 29 September, all operators, with the equipment they would be using on the operation, climbed aboard trucks and drove to New Sarum air force base for the final training jump. That night there were five free-fallers jumping from 12,000 feet onto the drop zone near our camp at Darwendale dam. The fifth jumper was a reserve who would take the place of anyone injured in the training jump. We jumped with a box in front of us containing two folding canoes, four paddles, a spare high-frequency radio with spare batteries for communication with Salisbury, two spare very high-frequency radios for short range communication, spare ammunition, food and water. The box was fitted with a twenty-eight-foot round reserve parachute and a barometric opening device arranged to open the canopy at 1,500 feet above the drop zone. I jumped with an AK rifle, AK chest webbing, belt order containing two water bottles, emergency rations, grenades, air-to-ground communication equipment and a small medical kit. Behind my legs I jumped

THE OPERATION THAT WENT RIGHT

Author in free-fall over Salisbury Rhodesia. *Camera* Dennis Croukamp

with my British army rucksack containing high-frequency radio and two batteries, di-pole antenna, very high-frequency radio and four batteries, five days' water, ten days' rations, lightweight sleeping bag, bivvie sheet to sleep under, a lightweight groundsheet, gas cooker, heavy knife, camouflage cream, toothbrush and one set of civilian clothing for escape purposes. Maps, codes, notebook, pencils, torch, matches, British passport and foreign currency I carried in my pockets. It was a realistic load and it took a dispatcher to help me kit up and move to the door prior to jumping because it was so heavy.

The aircraft we used was Jack Malloch's ancient DC-7.

The free-fall jump went off with no problems. Everyone landed safely and we got ready to bring in the twelve static-line jumpers. Our call sign commander, Major Wilson, established voice radio communication with the DC-7 as it was on jump-run below 1,000 feet. He ordered Jack to flash his landing lights once only and gave him course corrections: "Go left … roll out … steady … go right … roll out … steady," until the aircraft was aligned to the drop zone. Ten seconds before dropping, Wilson ordered, "Stand by the lights … red light on," then a pause followed by, "Green light on." The twelve static-line jumpers, using non-steerable canopies, tumbled out of the aircraft and landed safely. Captain MacKenzie landed at the water's edge, but it was only a foot deep so there was no danger.

The next few days were spent in refining canoe and inflatable-boat techniques, fine-tuning our equipment and having a final operational briefing. Up-to-date air photos showed a bend in the Chambeshi river which would be used as an indicator for the dispatcher whose task it was to drop us in the required position. Do bear in mind that this was all taking place in the days before global positioning systems. The only navigational equipment in the DC-7 would be a compass, the pilot Jack Malloch and our dispatcher using his Mk 1 eyeball out of the aircraft door. Everything had to be right first time.

The free-fall team was briefed for take-off on the evening of 3 October. Late that afternoon, dressed in the green uniforms we used on external raids, or 'externals', after a final briefing, kit check, radio check and test-firing of weapons, we climbed onto the truck and said our farewells to the men at the base camp. Arriving at New Sarum Air Force Base we went straight to the parachute school where we waited for darkness behind closed doors. Thirty minutes before take-off we were driven, with our two dispatchers, in an enclosed truck to the DC-7 which was parked at one end of the main runway, well out of sight.

Jack Malloch and his business partner, who would be in command as first pilot, welcomed us into the aircraft. The DC-7 had been fitted with a small number of passenger seats and a bank of oxygen cylinders with face masks and long plastic tubes reaching to the seating area. Jack explained that we would be taking off and climbing into the flightpaths used by cargo aircraft at an altitude of 18,000 to 19,000 feet above sea level. On radar we would be indistinguishable from any other cargo plane. We would fly north, over Tanzania, do a 180-degree turn and drop at 16,000 feet above the drop zone after about four hours in the air, most of it on oxygen.

The flight was uneventful. After a sharp 180-degree turn over Tanzania, I knew the jump was imminent. Kevin Milligan, the chief dispatcher, checked visibility out of the door and started shaking his head. There was a lot of haze down below, obscuring the features needed for identifying our drop zone.

The pilot opened the door to the cockpit and came into the cargo area. He

Author front extreme right, PJI Mike Witshire seated centre. *Photo* RhAF

spoke to Kevin who looked at his watch before returning to the cockpit. Kevin spoke to his assistant dispatcher and they both started to kit up, putting on their survival waistcoats, AK rifles and dispatcher parachutes. A few minutes later Kevin gave us the hand signal to 'kit up'.

I went across to my kit and checked the parachute, the KAP3 barometric automatic-opening device, the chest-mounted reserve, the red lamps on the altimeter plate, the chest webbing, the belt order, the AK rifle, my rucksack and the carrying straps it was trussed up in. All for the hundredth time that day. Slowly I put on my belt order, followed by my chest webbing. Then I got into the main parachute harness and adjusted the leg straps and chest strap. I stood in front of my rucksack and put my legs into the leg straps and connected the two quick-release hooks to my parachute harness chest straps. I tightened the straps to bring the rucksack as high up behind my legs as I could get it. Unfortunately it wasn't very far because my legs are short and the rucksack was huge. I found by bending my knees that the rucksack sat on the floor and took much of the weight off me. I then attached the chest-mounted reserve by the left-hand clip only. The assistant dispatcher placed my AK upside down on my left side and passed the attaching cord behind my neck and onto the right hand 'D' ring of the parachute harness. I clipped on the right-hand side of the reserve and the AK was in place. After attaching and tightening the side straps of the reserve to the parachute harness, I was ready. All this was done in an unpressurized aircraft, while wearing an oxygen mask at 18,000 feet or so. It was tiring.

The dispatchers checked everyone and their equipment before ordering us to, "Move to the door." We waddled in line towards the door. The box was already positioned at the edge of the door ready to be kicked out by the dispatchers. I was number three of four jumpers. We stood in front of the wide cargo door staring into the blackness of the night. Kevin was on his knees at the door, peering at the ground and speaking to the pilot on his microphone. I could see by how much he was shaking his head that all was not good and that he was having trouble identifying the bends in the river. He stood up and spoke to Major Wilson, who was number one to jump, and clearly imparted some bad news. Then I felt the aircraft rapidly lose height and watched the altimeter needle drop from 16,000 down to 12,000 and then 8,000 feet above ground level. I felt the plane execute a sharp 180-degree turn that nearly knocked me off my feet and noticed Kevin getting back onto his knees at the edge of the door. He was obviously having an animated conversation with the pilot and continued shaking his head. He took off his oxygen mask and looked up at Major Wilson. I could see him mouth the words "No go." Wilson turned back and as he was about to say something, Kevin received a message from the pilot. He suddenly leaned out the plane, pointed and shouted, "There it is! Go, go go!" He shouted so loudly I could hear him above the noise of the engines and slipstream. It was 0130 hours on the morning of 4 October 1979.

The dispatchers kicked the box out the door and helped us tumble into the slipstream. I have a distinct memory of flopping into the slipstream and being unable to 'drive out' with all that kit on. I remember seeing the black shadow of the plane disappear, smelling briefly the stink of the engines, realising that the roar of the engines had disappeared and relaxing into free-fall. I turned to face the two men and the box below me and I knew that the man behind me had done the same. I could clearly see the silver thread of the Chambeshi river winding across the grey bush in the moonlight and two black shadows in front and below me, that were Wilson and Cooke. I watched the needle of the altimeter unwind in the light of the red lamps on the altimeter plate. At 2,500 feet, indicated altitude above ground level, I got ready for 'pull'. I pulled at exactly 2,000 feet, 500 feet lower than I was supposed to, but I wanted to be close to the box when it opened and follow it closely to the ground. Without the box life would be difficult. My tactical assault parachute, made by GQ Company of UK, opened hard as usual and I was open slightly below 2,000 feet. I searched around for the white cross sewn on the top of the reserve canopy on the box. It was nowhere to be seen. I knew then that the box must have 'gone in'. The parachute on the box had not deployed.

I saw the other three canopies in the moonlight and followed the lowest towards the ground. The landing was uneventful among bush and small trees about six to eight feet high. The ground was rock hard, dry, grey and dusty. Immediately on landing, I extracted my rifle, loaded it and got my rucksack out of the carrying straps. I could fight and survive. My parachute, main and reserve, I stuffed down two antbear holes conveniently located and big enough to take all my kit. No digging needed.

The other three men were fairly well spread out but we all rendezvoused quickly despite the thick bush. We had practised this many times. Nobody had seen the box in the air or under canopy. It must have been smashed to a thousand pieces somewhere near us. Major Wilson ordered me to get the HF radio working and signal "No casualties on landing" and that we had lost the box. While I was tapping out the message in Morse code, he and one other set off to do a square search for the missing kit. This involved walking in ever-increasing squares outward from our base. They returned some time later with nothing to report. Instead of paddling by canoe to the targets, we would now have to walk. That would mean marching approximately 100 kilometres in four nights in addition to conducting the close-in reconnaissance on the bridges. This was a challenge.

The following day we rested in the laying-up position (LUP) and again, unsuccessfully, searched for the box. We listened carefully all day for any sounds which might indicate we had been spotted on entry but nothing untoward occurred. I made comms with base at 1800 hours on the HF radio as scheduled and 'read' them 'strength 5' which is as good as it gets. Using a patrol code of previously arranged letters and figures, I could come up on the air, pass a situation report and close down in less than two minutes. I was signalling at ten words per minute at over 600 kilometres to a radio station at Chirundu on the Rhodesian–Zambian border and was being monitored, again at 'strength 5', at Salisbury. This was farther than anyone had ever signalled before on operations.

Walking only at night, we reached the targets on the night of 6 October. It was a hard walk since we had to cross several tributaries flowing into the Chambeshi and avoid some small settlements. On reaching the bridges, we set up an LUP, or Laying Up Position, and Major Wilson, Lieutenant Cooke and Lance-Corporal Standish-White stripped off and swam to the bridges. I stayed and guarded the kit. At the bridges they detected the presence of an armed guard but went on to confirm the dimensions and the construction materials of the targets. As soon as they returned from the reconnaissance, we 'saddled up' and headed towards the general area of our drop zone. The following morning I made an unscheduled radio transmission confirming the dimensions of the targets, and confirmed the static-line drop in the early hours of 8 October. It took us the best part of another two nights to reach a suitable drop zone area for the rest of the team and to prepare for their arrival.

At approximately 0100 hours on the morning of 8 October, Major Wilson established communication with the aircraft carrying all our heavy kit and the twelve static-liners. The 'talk-in' of the aircraft went exactly as we had practised, the only difference being that we were talking to a South African pilot in a South African Air Force C-130 Hercules aircraft. The jump height was very low for a C-130, I would estimate between 400 and 500 feet, but everybody landed successfully. All the heavy kit had been palletized and came off the

THE OPERATION THAT WENT RIGHT

tailgate of the C-130, followed by the static-liners in one line.

The twelve new arrivals brought their personal kit into the rendezvous and we set about de-palletizing and centralizing the canoes, paddles, rubber boat, fuel, engine, explosives and parachutes. As we were digging a pit to bury all the pallets and 'chutes, a bush fire began moving towards us. It seemed some hunters were using the fire to drive game. Conveniently the hunters chased off after some game and left us to get on with our business. The fire was allowed to get close to our half-finished pit and all the 'jump' evidence was burnt to a cinder.

We set off in the canoes straight away, paddling upstream against the current towards the targets. I was paddling with Lance-Corporal Anton Grobler. Our boat had two rucksacks and rifles, both tied in, cordtex nets and cutting charges for the steel rail bridge. The boat was low down in the water with only four inches or so of freeboard. Paddling hard we could make, I would guess, about 4 kilometres per hour against the current. Before first light we moved into an LUP and hid our boats under trees and bush on the river bank.

The next night, 9 October, we encountered some rapids which we had not found in our recce. The river narrowed at this point, increasing speed severely over some big rocks. Anton and I paddled like mad and for thirty minutes or so it seemed we could not make any headway against the current. We put in a major effort and slowly began inching forward. For the four men in the rubber boat it was more difficult. They were forced to jettison one fifty-kilogram charge to avoid tipping the boat, before the carburettor took in some water, probably through fuel contamination due to the rolling of the boat. After paddling to the riverbank, Sergeant Vosloo stripped the carburettor, drained fuel from the top of the contaminated tank and restarted the motor: a sterling effort.

At the end of the first night we thankfully paddled into an LUP, a kilometre or so before the bridges. Again, we camouflaged the boats under trees and grass on the riverbank. A guard with a silenced weapon was on duty at all times. We could hear trains rumbling across the bridge during the day but there was no traffic at night.

The bridges were due to be rigged for demolition and blown on the night of 11 October. We needed three hours to rig the targets and during that time we had to hijack a suitable truck to make our escape south, towards a pick-up point within helicopter range of the Rhodesian border. When the moon rose on the evening of the 11th, we set off upstream in our canoes and rubber boat to the bridges. The skies were clouding over and a thunderstorm was developing. As we paddled, cloud cover increased, followed by thunder and lightning and then the rain. As we made our final turn on the river, about 300 metres from the bridges, a huge bolt of lightning lit the sky and illuminated the canoes and the bridges, with spray on the paddles seemingly frozen in time.

Rigging the bridges went like clockwork. Ropes were put around the concrete piers for the canoeists to hold on to. Wooden plaques, twelve inches square, were super-glued onto the piers to hold the cordtex nets and charges. This super-glue had been specially prepared for us and it was supplied in two plastic bottles: when the smaller bottle was poured into the bigger one we had ten seconds to pour it onto a plaque and stick it onto the concrete pier before it set rock solid. Anton and I had to offload cutting charges for the railway bridge and hand over cordtex nets to the rubber boat for them to install. Then we had to connect the explosive ring mains to the fifty-kilogram charges and the cordtex nets. Everything was duplicated wherever possible. There were two initiation sets to set the explosions off and two ring mains to distribute the shock waves to the explosive charges. We intended to drop two piers and three spans on each of the bridges. Whilst the charges were being prepared, desultory shooting developed on the northern side of the road bridge between some guards and some of the SAS operators who had been detailed to control traffic across the bridge.

Having completed our task, Anton and I paddled across to the southern bank of the concrete road bridge. There we disassembled our canoe and packed it away into its two bags. On the road we saw three trucks pulled up, each a rigid twenty-ton Mercedes loaded up with fertilizer destined for Lusaka from Dar es Salaam. They were ideal for our getaway and, more importantly, they had sufficient fuel. It seems that there were three brothers of Irish origin, born in Zambia, who operated these trucks running a convoy from Dar to Lusaka and back.

Truck number 1 had been waved through our checkpoint on the bridge. Number 2 was stopped, it being selected as the getaway truck. Number 1 returned to look for his number 2. Number 3 pitched up at that same moment. This was turning into a Marx Brothers movie. In addition to the three Zambian-Irish brothers, we collected their two African drivers and, if I remember correctly, two white Zambian boys, a birthday boy and his chum who was along for the ride. In order that we should not be compromised, we had to take them with us.

THE OPERATION THAT WENT RIGHT

We piled onto the back of the getaway truck and threw out all the fertilizer bags except the ones around the edge of the vehicle. The Irish-Zambian owner insisted on driving. We loaded our six canoes, the rubber boat, our personal kit, our seven 'guests' and all sixteen of us as soon as Sergeant-Major Fisher initiated the time delays. We had fifteen minutes before the bridges blew. While driving south, we soon heard the *CRRRUMP* and felt the shock wave as the charges detonated. It was about 0200 hours on the morning of 12 October. Telephone wires were also cut, to prevent interference from the Zambian authorities.

It was a fairly uneventful drive down the Great North Road and we encountered no opposition. Our Irish-Zambian driver knew the area well and was very helpful. As day dawned, we entered the Luangwa South national park. Although we were seen by locals, our vehicle attracted little attention since no one could see into the back. We laid up after first light and I established comms with base. The code word came back that our op had been 100 per cent successful. However, the pressure was still on and we had to find a landing zone for our helicopter pick-up.

After a fair amount of 'bundu-bashing' in the truck we arrived at a LUP, approximately 250 kilometres from the Rhodesian border. I got on the radio again and we had uplift confirmed for early the following morning.

Next morning, 13 October, base again confirmed that we had two Bell helicopters on the way to our location. The Bell 205s, or Hueys, and known as Cheetahs by the Rhodesians, have two large rotor blades that make a highly distinctive *whap whap* noise that can be heard up to fifteen kilometres away. At a prearranged time, Major Wilson put out a continuous transmission on his VHF radio which the choppers homed in on. On landing, the chopper technicians unloaded fuel drums and pumps and refuelled the helicopters. Within fifteen minutes we were airborne, back to 'Bright Lights', beer and some well earned R&R.

On arrival at Salisbury, we learned that our Zambian guests were being well looked after by Special Branch and that they were later helicoptered onto a road in Zambia once all the fuss had died down.

A few days after we got back to camp, Jack Malloch turned up to invite the free-fallers to his office for a few drinks that afternoon. His secretary opened up his office fridge as we got stuck into a few cold beers. Jack began by saying that as he watched us jump from the DC-7, he "never expected to see us again". We all laughed. The conversation ranged over his aircraft operation, his flying career and his love of the DC-7 and his new project the Mk XXI Spitfire,

Jack Malloch's Spitfire Mk2I. *Private collection*

which he was going to test-fly once he had located some 20mm cannons. Only then would it be "complete". He said he intended to fly it into a contact. Those few drinks closed the door, so to speak, on an operation that was a complete success, and one where we returned with virtually all the equipment that we started with. That doesn't happen often in war.

As mentioned earlier, Jack died a few months later. He was flying his Spitfire on a photo-shoot west of Salisbury when the aircraft went into a cloud and disappeared from the view of the chase aircraft. The Spitfire flew straight into the ground. Gone but never, ever, forgotten.

To complete this account of Op Cheese, it would be useful to have a perspective from the air force. I am indebted to Kevin Milligan, the senior RhAF dispatcher on the operation, for writing down his memories. Kevin later became a Squadron Leader and OC Parachute Training School …

… As early as May 1979, Jack Malloch's DC-7 was to be found regularly parked at the far end of 3 Squadron hard standing. Resplendent in its camouflage, it dwarfed the Dakotas. We would use it for special operational training and for operations. By this time I had been appointed as Operations Officer and was briefed that there was a requirement to do some training jumps with a free-fall team and twenty static-line troops with large boxes of equipment, from the DC-7.

The SAS plus some large boxes were duly loaded onto the aircraft and off we went. We had been dropping boxes using static line for some time, but these were larger than normal. The DZ was also unusual as it was sited alongside Darwendale dam, about thirty-kilometres outside Salisbury. We had planned a free-fall drop first but this had to be aborted due to too much air traffic approaching Salisbury airport, but we were cleared for the static-line drop. We ran in low level alongside the dam and dispatched the first load of boxes. All went well and then we commenced the second run-in.

In preparation for the drop and because we knew the boxes were larger than in the past, we had removed both cargo doors to give us as much space as possible. Because the box was so long we were concerned about it twisting and jamming in the door as we dispatched it. We had come up with the idea of mounting a wooden ramp in the door that would extend into the slipstream. The box would be positioned on the ramp inside the aircraft and then, on the green [light], we could give it a mighty heave to send it down the ramp and on its way. We had everything ready as we ran in and were prepared to give it a good shove. The green came on and we pushed it out down the ramp but it twisted in the slipstream and jammed against the doorframe and would go no further. There was moment of panic as we overshot the DZ and struggled to bring it back inside. Finally we managed to wrestle it back into the fuselage. We set it up again as the aircraft made another run-in. The green came on and this time with everyone giving a mighty push, it just cleared the frame and out into the slipstream. We heaved a sigh of relief but it was obvious that it was not the best of plans. We circled again, the ramp was cleared out of the way and we dispatched the troops. It was rather windy by this time and there were some brisk landings. We returned to base very pensive. I did not know what was in the box that it had to be so large—the less one knew about secret operations the better—but our method of dispatching it was not very suitable. I thought the SAS might have to pack their loads into smaller boxes.

Sometime later we did a training jump for the free-fall team before we were stood down till 10 September. Then we dispatched the team and their equipment box, twice from 15,000 feet using the Dakota DC-3. On the first jump, the team watched in amazement as the parachute on the box opened in front of them as they passed through 10,000 feet. The parachute pack had torn open. On the second jump, the box the SAS planned to use was too large for a clean exit through the door. The free-fall team jumped anyway and Frank Hales and I followed them. I was using a Strato Cloud ram air canopy which was packed in a piggyback system with the reserve mounted on the back as well as the main. It was a very compact and comfortable system. It also had a simple method of canopy release called a three-ring release. It entailed pulling one handle to effect the canopy release and then the reserve handle. At 2,500 feet I pulled as normal but as it deployed I immediately found myself being rotated in a tight turn that was building up to a spin. The canopy had malfunctioned and I rapidly went through my new cutaway drills to release the canopy and then pulled my reserve ripcord. The system worked well and I had a good ride down on the steerable reserve.

Generally, things did not seem to be going well in preparation for whatever the SAS were scheming. A little later Frank Hales called me into his office and briefed me that the trials and rehearsals were in preparation for a major operation and that it was set for 12 September. It was of the utmost importance that it succeed. Operation Uric had been carried out recently to bring pressure to bear on Mozambique but now it was time to strike at Zambia. The operation was to be codenamed 'Cheese'.

Zambia had two major routes for her imports/exports: one to the south through Rhodesia and the other to the north to Dar es Salaam, Tanzania, utilizing the 'Tan-Zam' rail link. It was crucial to their economy. It was also being heavily used by ZIPRA to transport their war equipment and men to Lusaka from where they would infiltrate into Rhodesia. It was in Rhodesia's interests to force President Kaunda's hand so he would become dependent on the southern route through Rhodesia where economic pressure could be brought to bear. Miltary Intelligence had long since discerned that the most effective way to do this was to destroy the massive Chambeshi rail bridge and its sister road bridge only 100 metres away. The bridges straddled the Chambeshi River and were sited in the northeast of Zambia, south of the Tanzanian border. They were nearly 750 kilometres from Salisbury. The rail bridge was the longest one in Africa. The distances were daunting to say the least and soldiers had never been dropped in so deep before. They would be totally alone and beyond reach of help; however, so important was the task that the challenges had to be accepted. The destruction of the bridges would also cause explosive political repercussions and so this had resulted in the operation being put on hold. Finally, however, the situation was such that by August 1979, the SAS was given the green light.

The final plan was agreed. A team of four SAS would do a night high-altitude low-opening (HALO) jump, move up to the bridges, carry out a reconnaissance of the bridges and assess the defences. They would then locate a

THE OPERATION THAT WENT RIGHT 125

DZ and call in an assault team, complete with boats and explosives. They were to be dropped at low level by night. The party would then move downstream, capture and destroy the bridges before exfiltrating to an LZ for helicopter uplift. This in itself would mean hijacking a suitable vehicle, then driving about 200 kilometres through Zambian territory to a point close enough to Rhodesia to be within range of the Bell 205 'Cheetah' helicopters; and all this while being hunted by the Zambian military which would of course be aware by then of the sabotage. The indomitable Major Grahame Wilson would be the mission commander and if anyone could pull it off, he and his carefully selected men could. As the only man in the security forces to have been awarded the Grand Cross of Valour, the Silver Cross and the Bronze Cross, he had already established a formidable reputation within a unit renowned for its extraordinary achievements against all the odds.

Frank advised me that Grahame had already flown to the area of the bridges in the DC-7 to select a suitable DZ. There was a lot of haze and it had taken two separate flights before a suitable spot could be selected for their insertion. It was located close to a prominent bend in the river which would make a good 'indicating point' (IP) in the moonlight. Unfortunately, it was downstream of the target, meaning a tougher paddle, but Grahame found that acceptable under the circumstances. The DC-7 would be used as it regularly overflew Zambian airspace on cargo runs to countries north of Zambia and would arouse less suspicion. It was clear to me that this was going to be the most spectacular operation I had been involved with, as well as possibly the most important of the war to date. It was to prove to be the most interesting and challenging too, but I didn't know that at the time.

On the morning of 12 September, Frank Hales, myself and Mike Duffy lifted off in the DC-7. We had on board a box packed to the same size as the SAS HALO team would require and the parachute pack had been reinforced. The team were not present as they were finalizing all their equipment for the operation. We climbed to 10,000 feet and Frank directed the aircraft over the DZ before giving us the thumbs-up. We heaved the box clearly out of the door and followed after it. We made a formation around the box as it plummeted towards the DZ, its pilot 'chute trailing, preventing it from tumbling. We pulled at our set heights then looked down to see the box under canopy and drifting down to the DZ. It had worked perfectly.

Once it was dark, the SAS team, comprising Grahame, Lieutenant Phil Cooke, Andrew 'Stan' Standish-White and Russell Tiffin, arrived with their equipment. We reviewed the situation with Grahame and the pilots and then got underway. Tension was very high when we finally reached the Chambeshi river and Frank anxiously scanned below for the IP, the place on the ground that would confirm our position, but try as he might, the haze was so bad that he had to abort the mission. The disappointment was palpable on the long flight home. It was so frustrating after all the preparations.

Grahame agreed that the only option was to wait for the next moon period and try again. We arranged training jumps for the HALO, or free-fall, team on 25, 26 and 27 September, all of them from the Dakota as the DC-7 was not available. Paul French, recently returned from a Mortar Instructors Course at the School of Infantry, who had replaced Russell Tiffin in the team, much to Russell's chagrin, recalls that also on 27 September the HALO and assault party rolled out of camp to a secret training area near Darwendale dam and set up camp. Major Wilson then briefed them on the operation. The operators were hushed as the plan unfolded and the men realized that no one had been on operations so deep in enemy territory before. They did not even have proper maps, being given only photocopies from a Zambian Tourist Board map. They were to be used in the event of escape and evasion being necessary. It was pointed out that there could be no casualty evacuation until the end of the operation. They would be out on a limb with only their own resources to sustain them.

The HALO team would do a night jump onto a DZ about forty kilometres from target, complete with two canoes and all the necessary kit. This included ten days' rations, five days' water, radios, batteries, weapons and ammo. It was because of the collapsible Klepper folding canoes that the box they had been training with was so large. They would canoe upstream by night to the bridges, carry out a reconnaissance, return to the drop zone and then talk in by radio another aircraft with the assault team. The assault team of twelve men, commanded by Captain Bob MacKenzie, would parachute in at low level, complete with one ton of demolitions, canoes, one Zodiac inflatable boat with silenced motor and rations. They would then all travel upriver to target, secure the two bridges, and set and blow their explosive charges.

Grahame had various options for exfiltration. Plan A was to hijack a suitable truck at the road bridge and then drive the team to Luangwa Valley South. That would be close enough for the Bells to reach them and get them out. Simple! Intense rehearsals followed and Paul and Stan constructed a scale model of the bridges based on aerial photos taken recently by the 'Blues' (air force personnel). Many hours were spent canoeing on the dam and placing specially prepared charges on a partially submerged old farmhouse. This included the use of special cordtex nets, like a plastic clothes line with explosive in the centre, which would make the demolition more effective.

The final training jump, a dress rehearsal, was carried out on the night of 29 September. Frank Hales, Mike Duffy and I had the parachutes ready for them when they arrived at the hangar. There were five free-fallers, as one would be reserve in case of injury. They had the equipment box containing two canoes, four paddles, spare HF radio and batteries, two spare VHF radios, ammo, food and water. We prepared the box with a parachute, a strobe light (a very bright flashing light) and a Kap 3 automatic-opening device, while the men kitted up. We loaded up the DC-7 and then took off for Darwendale in the moonlight. We kitted up the free-fallers with their rucksacks on the climb to altitude and the loads were heavy. Paul French has commented that he jumped with his AK-47 and a mass of equipment. In his rucksack he carried an HF Morse code radio and all the ancillaries needed for special operations communicating (on the actual op he also carried his British Passport and foreign currency). It was a staggering load and I was in awe of the guys. Both Mike and I helped him kit up and move to the door before the jump.

We ran in over the dam at 12,000 feet as we were not using oxygen. Frank did the 'spotting' by looking out of the door and giving the pilot course corrections to steer the aeroplane to the point at which the paratroopers would be dispatched. He gave the signal and we heaved the box out of the door, followed immediately by the free-fallers. Lieutenant Phil Cooke had some excitement on opening when he realized he had a malfunction. He carried out his drills superbly and made a safe landing on his reserve. As soon as they grouped around the box, which had worked well, Major Wilson talked in the aircraft and static-line troops. By now we had descended to low level and were running in. The pilot gave a quick flash of the landing lights to orientate Grahame who talked us in by giving the pilot course corrections. Bob MacKenzie was standing ready with his assault team. As always, the former American airborne veteran was wearing his distinctive US-pattern paratroop helmet. It was always easy to pick him out and I never saw him use anything else. He was a great character, very courageous and a truly professional soldier. His men showed him the utmost loyalty. As the green came on, Mike and I rapidly dispatched them. I hoped that Grahame's assessment of the wind drift was correct and that the lads would be clear of the water. In the event, they were, except one. Bob found himself splashing down on the water's edge but fortunately it was only knee-deep. He was soaked, not very happy, but unharmed. We peeled off and returned to base at New Sarum, glad that it had gone well.

Two days later Frank called me into his office. He explained that he had booked a well-deserved leave to South Africa some time earlier and as much as he would have loved to be in on the operation, he could not disappoint his wife by postponing the holiday. I would be in charge of Op Cheese from the PTS point of view. Grahame was in the picture. I was proud that he trusted me and terrified at the same time. I don't think I had a decent night's sleep from that day until the assault party was finally dropped.

On the morning of 2 October, I was informed by Grahame that we would be going that night on an air reconnaissance to Chambeshi to assess the haze and moonlight conditions. We would use a 5 Squadron Canberra. This was definitely a first for us. The Canberras regularly carried out clandestine flights over Zambia and Mozambique taking aerial photographs but not with parachute jumping instructors (PJIs) to 'eyeball' the situation. When Jack did it in his DC-7 he used his air cargo story for Lusaka tower. I think in this case it was say nothing and just do it. The chances of interception by enemy MiG fighters or missiles were deemed slight. The pilot to take us was the OC himself, Squadron Leader Rowe. He briefed us that we would fly at 35,000 feet before dropping down to the proposed drop height of 15,000 feet over target. We squeezed ourselves into the jet bomber and off we went. We cruised over Zambia at high level then began our descent over the target area. Grahame slid back from the bomb aimer's position and gestured for me to move up. I squeezed into position with some difficulty as I was wearing my aircrew parachute and then looked down through the Perspex dome. We circled and even though it was hazy I could discern the Chambeshi river in the moonlight. I slid back into the cockpit and gave Grahame the thumbs-up. We quickly returned to 35,000 feet and New Sarum where we agreed it was 'all systems go' for the next evening, 3 October.

On the day of our departure I was going over my aerial photos and preparing myself for the operation. It was then that I heard the bad news about an incident that day. A few days prior to this, on Operation Miracle, I had dispatched Rhodesian Light Infantry (RLI) troops into the New Chimoio terrorist camp in Mozambique which turned into an extended fight. Following this, Hawker Hunter and Canberra aircraft were requested to carry out airstrikes on a Frelimo column that appeared to be readying itself for a reprisal raid against a security base at Ruda in the Rhodesian Eastern Districts. In the ensuing action both a Canberra and Hunter were downed by severe ground fire. It was a costly blow that rattled the Blues.

I was glad that I would be in a DC-7 at 15,000 feet beyond reach of most ground fire and also that our insertion would be very clandestine. There was little time to dwell on it as once it was dark the SAS arrived, as did the pilots. As usual Squadron Leader George 'Punchy' Alexander would be captain and Flight Lieutenant Jack Malloch the co-pilot. They had been the crew for the training jumps and we were in very good hands. George, a Greek-Rhodesian and a former OC of 3 Squadron, was a very good and decorated pilot but rather volatile at times, hence the nickname. Jack, a well-built man who oozed a quiet confidence, was a legend in his own right and had carried out many daring exploits in his time. He had flown Spitfires in the Second World War. Nothing ever fazed him. The men found him considerate and amusing. His big passion at that time was to restore a Spitfire from its plinth as gate guardian at New Sarum air force base and fly it once more. He achieved this ambition.

We reviewed the plan and thirty minutes before take-off, we loaded the aircraft in readiness. The meteorological forecast was not too good with regards to ground haze and I went over my photos again as I taped them to the inside of the fuselage near the door. Mike Duffy, who would once more be the oxygen NCO, was busy fussing over the bottles as the team settled down for the long flight. Grahame managed to look nonchalant as always; his calmness no doubt reassured the rest of the lads.

The four large radial engines on the DC-7 fired up in a throaty roar and I once more looked at the long, blue flames from the exhaust stacks. During the day one could not see them but at night they looked like bonfires to me. At that stage in the war we were very concerned regarding heat-seeking SAM-7 missiles. We taxied out on to the main runway and at 2330 hours George poured on the power and we rumbled off for target. In accordance with the plan we climbed to 18,000 feet and followed the normal air-lane route over Zambia towards Tanzania. We sat back, oxygen masks on, because the aircraft was unpressurized and contemplated the task ahead. Mike made regular checks on us to make sure no one was suffering from lack of oxygen, which was the last thing we would need. At the appointed time, George brought us around and began to descend to drop height at 15,000 feet above ground level. Mike and I were kept very busy assisting the guys to fit their kit and the heavily loaded rucksacks. This was no easy task but everyone knew the routine well and final checks were carried out.

The free-fall box was positioned in the door, the box's pilot 'chute static line hooked up and the Kap 3 automatic-opening device was armed. The men closed up towards the box. I dropped to my knees and positioned myself at the door, looking down over the door sill straight ahead. It was very hazy once more and I knew George was relying on his instruments and dead reckoning for our positioning. He did not have the sophisticated navigation aids so common today. Nevertheless, I knew he would make a good job in positioning for an accurate run in from the IP. He informed me were commencing run-in and try as I might, I could not see the river, the bend or anything I could use as my IP for run-up to target. George insisted that, according to his dead reckoning, we must be over target. I did not doubt him but was equally insistent that I could not see it. For static-line drops, the captain has command of the aircraft for the drop. For free-fall, it is the No. 1 dispatcher who does the 'spotting' or visual confirmation of aircraft position over the ground and who has command. Only the 'spotter' can see accurately whether or not they are directly over the DZ.

When we had obviously flown past the DZ, I stood up and told Grahame about the problem and suggested a run-in at 12,000 feet. He agreed and George brought the aircraft around hard on a reverse-course run. I took the air photograph of the DZ off the wall of the aircraft and reversed it to make sure I was properly orientated. I scanned the ground below, or more properly the haze, through the darkness for a glimpse of anything I might recognize, but no joy. George was becoming very insistent but I could not pick up any landmarks. Like Frank Hales before me, I was not prepared to put the team at extra risk and was prepared to accept his anger and abort the mission if necessary.

We agreed to a final run at 8,000 feet. It was make or break. I knew how hard it must have been on the lads as they stood weighed down by their kit and nerves stretched to the limits. (I recently asked Stan how he felt as we circled around, getting lower on each run in. He said, "I had forgotten all about the circling; I was so *poep*-scared [shit-scared] it was not surprising.") I caught Grahame's eye and he gave me a nod of assurance. As we turned and began our final run-in, I was very aware that the DC-7 must sound very noisy at 8,000 feet above ground level. To go any lower would risk compromising the operation. We were already pushing our luck.

I frantically peered out of the door for any sign of the river and the crucial bend in the river that would confirm our ground position. To my great disappointment, once again I could see nothing. With a very heavy heart I told George to abort and indicated to Grahame to stand back from the door. I was so angry and frustrated when George said, "It must be there!" Only good discipline prevented me from saying something that I would regret. I had a final look out of the door.

It was like something out of a movie. At just the right time and at just the right angle, I saw the moon glinting on the river bend that I was looking for, just as it was in the photo. There was little time for the normal flat-turn corrections on run-in as I called to George, "Come left … come left … harder … steady," then, "Go, go, go" to Grahame. It wasn't very textbook. The strobe light on the box was switched on and Mike and I forced the box out of the door. We then helped the guys as they waddled to the door and plunged out into the darkness. The time was 0130 hours on 4 October. Operation Cheese was finally underway.

Mike and I were ecstatic and so relieved to have seen and dispatched them successfully over target. Now came the excruciating wait before the team radioed us to confirm how the drop had gone. The DC-7 went into a wide orbit well clear of the area but within range of Grahame's voice radio.

Stan remembers, "My exit was horrendous." Paul remembers, because of his heavy kit, just flopping into the slipstream, the brief smell of the engines and then the silence of the free-fall. As he turned to face the box he could clearly see the moon glinting on the river and the dark shapes of Grahame and Phil below him. He followed them down to pull height and opened the parachute at 2,000 feet as he wanted to be close to the box. He searched for the white cross sewn on to the top of the canopy as a marker but he could not pick it up. He could see the other three canopies though and steered towards the lowest, Major Wilson's. He landed among some small bushes and trees and quickly armed himself. After shoving his parachutes down two large antbear holes, he rendezvoused with the others. All was well but no one had seen the box under canopy. Stan recalls, "Our group was pretty messy; the box just thundered down." Grahame contacted Jack on his radio and informed us with the code word that the drop was good. We did not know then that the box was missing. We turned for home. Grahame meanwhile organized a square search for the box. This involved two men walking in ever-increasing squares but it was fruitless. Paul then tapped out a signal to the forward listening station at Kariba, informing them of the situation. Next morning they carefully searched through the bush once more but had no luck. It did not look good. Grahame says that it confirmed their standard operating procedures whereby items of importance were carried on the parachutist and not in a box. They would have to change their plan of canoeing to the bridges and instead proceed on foot. They laid up for the rest of the day and all was quiet. It would seem that their insertion had thankfully gone unnoticed.

That evening they began their long hard walk to the bridges. Time was of the essence but so was stealth. Of course, as we flew back, I only knew that the jump had gone well and that they were on target. When Mike and I landed at Salisbury we were weary but very relieved. I don't think George was too happy with me but Jack seemed in good humour as well he should be. The next day, when I returned to Parachute Training School, I discovered from OC Flying Wing that the box was missing and the reconnaissance was proceeding on foot. Consequently, Phase Two would be delayed.

Major Wilson and his men made good progress towards the bridges, finally reaching a wide tributary that joined the Chambeshi river on the night of 6 October. They were very close now. Paul remained in the LUP guarding the kit, while the other three stripped off and swam to the bridges. All was quiet as they carried out their reconnaissance, noting with satisfaction that it was just as they had expected from the photos and the models. The explosives being brought in would be more than sufficient for the task. As anticipated, there was a small police presence guarding the bridges. Very satisfied with the recce, they slipped away undetected and re-joined Paul who sent an unscheduled radio transmission confirming the dimensions of the bridges and confirmed the static-line drop to be carried out early on 8 October. They moved off and returned to the area of their DZ. They found a suitable DZ for the rest of the team and awaited their arrival.

On the morning of 6 October, OC Flying Wing told me to report to Fylde, the secret airfield near Hartley, with one other dispatcher, in preparation for the assault party which had already pre-positioned there. Fylde was hardly ever mentioned and only then by those in the know and in hushed tones. I knew of it but had never been there. It was sited in a very rural area about forty kilometres west of Salisbury. Mike Duffy and I set off by road. Imagine our amazement upon arrival to see a South African Air Force C-130 Hercules. I had dispatched South African Reconnaissance Commando troops from our Dakotas into the 'Russian Front' in Gaza province, southern Mozambique on occasion, as recently they had been working hand in hand with the SAS. But I never expected this! The C-130 is a magnificent transport aircraft and can

THE OPERATION THAT WENT RIGHT   133

carry over sixty paras and is also ideal for parachuting cargo off its ramp at the rear. It was the answer to our prayers for dropping the bigger loads. Someone in high places had obviously pulled strings. It was in South Africa's interest to have Kenneth Kaunda, president of Zambia, reigned in, as terrorists were using Zambia as a base.

We met up with the crew which was comprised of the captain, Major Gardner, an ebullient man who could not have been more enthusiastic or helpful, the co-pilot, navigators, engineers, two loadmasters and two parachute dispatchers, and checked over all the pallets, sixty-four-foot parachutes and resupply equipment. The C-130 was going to be used to parachute in the twelve men plus a Zodiac inflatable boat with motor, fuel, six canoes, a dozen or so paddles and about a ton of explosives, detonators, cordtex, initiating sets and so on. Now I understood why the boxes had been so big for the trials from the DC-7. As the majority of the SAS was unfamiliar with the aircraft, the captain explained the various characteristics, aircraft drills and emergency drills. The parachute dispatchers, along with me and Mike, then took the SAS for some synthetic ground training to practise the techniques. I had jumped the C-130 several times in the UK with the British Parachute Regiment which definitely helped.

The training posed no problems and the men rapidly familiarized themselves with the new drills. After discussions with Bob MacKenzie, the team commander, and Major Gardner, we decided to do two training jumps. The first would be without equipment and the second would be with full kit. During this time, two dispatchers who had arrived from 3 Air Supply Platoon, Rhodesian Army and the loadmasters were considering and preparing the best means of palletizing all the equipment.

Sometime later, Bob MacKenzie was informed that the deployment would not take place that night. This was fortunate as the high winds throughout the day had prevented any training jumps and it would give more time for rigging of the pallets.

The next day, at 1500 hours, all the pallets were rigged. An hour later the huge aircraft took off and ran in at 600 feet over the airfield. On board was a pallet rigged with three fuel drums which we wanted to use as a trial drop. The C-130 ran in over the DZ, the loadmasters dispatched the pallet over the ramp at the rear of the aircraft and the pallet slid over the tailgate, with the sixty-four-foot-diameter parachute rapidly deploying in the slipstream. The winds were quite strong and as the pallet landed a few moments later, it hit hard before being rolled over. The large parachute was caught by the wind before collapsing. We ran over to the load and saw that the drums had sustained substantial damage. When we discussed it with the loadmasters after the C-130 had landed, they said that it was not uncommon; it was realized that if the pallet carrying the Zodiac rolled on landing, the damage could be quite extensive. The assault group leader decided that in calmer conditions, which were more prevalent at night, the risk would be warranted.

At 1800 hours that day, the winds were calmer and we emplaned the paratroopers for a familiarization jump without equipment. We used Rhodesian parachutes which the SAS had collected from New Sarum. We had fourteen paratroopers but only twelve would be going on the operation. I guess the chance to jump a C-130 was too good an opportunity to miss. We would be dispatching seven from each door, port and starboard. The Dakota and DC-7 have doors only on the port side, so jumping from the starboard door would mean adopting a mirror-image stance for aircraft and exit drills. The men had no problems with this.

We ran in at 600 feet and the men were looking very pleased with themselves as they prepared to jump from this lovely aircraft. Mike and I were positioned, one at each door, along with the two parachute dispatchers. The green light came on and the men were on their way in a fast, compact group, surprising even the parachute dispatchers. Since they were jumping without kit and with both port and starboard doors used simultaneously, grouping in the air was extremely close, with some canopies even touching. This led to all the troops landing very close together, ensuring rapid rendezvous procedures. There were no injuries and the SAS were delighted with the C-130. This was something different for everyone's logbooks and provided a bit of one-upmanship over their buddies.

All the men were in good humour but obviously apprehensive as they kitted up later for the real thing. There had not been time for another training jump but the first had gone so well that they were full of confidence in themselves, the aircraft and its crew, which were first class. The four pallets with all of the heavy equipment were loaded and final briefings were carried out. Over 800 kilometres away, Major Wilson and his team were eagerly awaiting their arrival.

At 2330 hours Major Gardner brought the four turboprop engines on the C-130 up to full power, moved swiftly down the runway and lifted off. Phase Two was underway. The winds were calm and we had a decent moon. The route to the bridges was made at 28,000 feet. The aircraft was pressurized so there was no need for oxygen sets. The men, in their terrorist 'greens', faces and hands darkened with camo cream, some with RPD light machine guns, some with AK-47s, sat quietly, some dozing, as we flew north. Sergeant Vossy Vosloo looked relaxed. Little did he know that he was to later play a key part in the success of the operation.

As we flew on, I began to think about the time, a few years before, when I was working on a mine on the Zambian Copperbelt. I had formed a skydiving club at Mufulira and used to fly to different towns in Zambia to do display parachute jumps into trade fairs and agricultural shows. Once when we were jumping into the Ndola Trade Fair, we kept President Kenneth Kaunda waiting for ten minutes as we flew to the arena. It was a timing mistake on the part of the organizers and as they realized their error, they frantically tried to contact us to bring the timings forward. We could not fly there any faster and there was not enough time to bring another show into the arena so the president twiddled his thumbs. The jump went very well but not many people can say that they kept a president waiting: a dubious honour. I never could have dreamed then that I would be flying back into Zambia on a mission like this.

My reminiscences were interrupted when one of the dispatchers came over and informed me that we were to begin our descent to low level. The pilot began a rapid descent and then the aircraft was depressurized as we levelled out. Bob MacKenzie looked my way and I gave him the thumbs-up. He gave me a nod and a big smile as I gave the command to stand up and check equipment. The men carried out their drills and the dispatchers opened the parachute doors at the rear of the aircraft. We could smell the African night air as we took up our positions in the door. Down below I could vaguely see the dark outline of the bush as we approached the DZ. I remembered being shot at on several occasions such as this and thought if just one stray round was to strike the detonators, we would all be history. Fortunately all was very quiet on the ground. Grahame had voice communications with Major Gardner and directed us in. The red light to stand in the door came on and the first men on each side took up their stand-in-the-door positions. They did not know what lay ahead but no matter what happened they were determined to give it their best shot. The green light, the executive order to jump, came on and I yelled out to Bob, "Go and 2 and 3 and 4 and 5 … " until the entire stick was gone. We hauled in the static lines and trailing bags as the aircraft pulled away.

A short while later, Grahame came up on the radio and informed Major

Gardner that the drop had gone well. He requested us to orbit while the parachutists cleared the DZ before we dropped the pallets. We made a wide orbit and the ramp was lowered. The loadmasters busied themselves with the final preparations as Grahame talked us in at 600 feet. The pilot quickly reacted to his corrections and then steadied on target. The green light came on and the loadmasters sent the four pallets thundering down the rollers and over the tailgate. The parachutes streamed out, landing in a tight group on the DZ. Grahame radioed that the drop was spot on. The aircraft climbed away, returning high level to Fylde.

I felt as happy as a dog with two tails. After all the tribulations, everything had gone incredibly smoothly. Now it was up to the SAS. I knew that they would succeed no matter what the odds. These very men had been through it all before on Operation Uric when they had destroyed the bridges at Barragem in Mozambique. We landed at 0300 hours and I bedded down in our vehicle for the rest of the night. I slept well, only to be wakened by Mike Duffy much later. It was already well into the morning and the C-130 would soon be returning to South Africa. We had of course taken the precaution of bringing our free-fall parachutes with us. We said our very grateful thanks to all the crew and then boarded the C-130 with them. Major Gardner, obliging as always, climbed out to 8,000 feet then turned in over Fylde. Mike and I were like two little boys, so excited were we as we launched ourselves off the ramp for a wonderful free-fall skydive. It was the perfect way to round off our part in the operation.

Of course, for Major Wilson and his intrepid bunch the job was only just beginning. I was to hear their story later. After the assault party had rendezvoused with Grahame, they gathered in all their kit. A pit was being dug to bury the pallets and parachutes when a bush fire, which had been started by hunters to flush out game, swept their way. After the hunters moved on, there was a scramble to get the explosives and kit clear of the fire whilst allowing it to destroy the parachutes and pallets. They moved down to the river and began their paddle in six very heavily loaded canoes and the Zodiac inflatable boat. They laid up before first light, hiding their boats under the heavy bush lining the bank. The next night was the most troublesome as they continued upstream towards their goal. The river narrowed and they had to paddle with all their strength to make any headway through the rock-strewn rapids. The going was much slower than they anticipated and progress was slow. The canoeists were giving it their all, at the same time wishing they were in the Zodiac with its silenced 15hp motor. Bob McKenzie and his team of three in the boat were, however, having their own problems. The Zodiac, heavily laden like the canoes, was extremely low in the water and was responding like a drunken whale as it ploughed on. The craft was being rocked and bounced as it struggled through the rapids until finally they found themselves spinning out of control and carried downstream for some distance. They tried again, in vain. Bob, as a last resort, had to make the decision to jettison some of the special charges. They still would have enough to destroy the main piers of the bridges. On the third attempt they succeeded in breaching the rushing waters.

To compound the situation, just as they were congratulating themselves on making it through the rapids, the motor cut out. They had just switched over to the last fuel tank which was contaminated with water. They made it to the riverbank while Grahame and his 'Cockleshell heroes' paddled on, oblivious to the drama unfolding behind them. Bob knew the situation was critical. How could they get the charges to the bridges? Sergeant Vosloo came to the rescue. In true adept SAS fashion, he stripped and cleaned the carburettor before draining the valuable uncontaminated fuel from the tank. They crossed fingers, tried the starter and the motor sputtered into life. They got under way again. Vossy was the hero of the moment and that seemed to spell the end of their troubles.

By the night of 10 October, they had laid up just a short distance from the bridges and could hear the traffic passing over. Grahame and Bob reviewed the respective tasks with the team. Every man knew what was expected of him. Darkness fell and after waiting for a couple of hours they set off. It was raining and stormy. Just as they approached the bridges, there was a brilliant flash of lightning. The whole scene was immediately bathed in bright light, revealing the giant rail bridge before them in all its detail. It was a sight they will not forget. Luckily, it did not prompt any adverse reaction and they pressed on.

Upon reaching the bridges, there was a myriad of tasks to be performed and each call sign set about it with the perfection that comes from a well-rehearsed plan. Charges were set on both bridges and Lieutenant Phil Cook and his men set about hijacking a truck on the road bridge. There was short exchange of shots with a policeman who had come to investigate before he ran off into the night. A police roadblock sign, which they brought with them, was set up. Vehicles were allowed to pass until finally a suitable twenty-ton truck loaded with fertilizer was stopped. It was being driven by a white man of Irish descent, accompanied by his black co-driver. It would be ideal for the getaway. The roadblock sign was replaced with breakdown triangles so that other vehicles could proceed, but a similar truck pulled up to render help to the 'breakdown'. Just then, a truck which had a short time before passed to the south, returned to the bridge. The driver was the brother of the truck driver who had been hijacked. It transpired that it was custom to travel in convoy and render each other support when needed. He refused to leave his brother, as did the other truck driver. To complicate the situation even further, they were accompanied by a ten-year-old boy and a young friend who were coming along for the ride as part of a birthday treat. Was he in for a treat! Yet another truck was pulling up. It was becoming something of a theatrical farce as by this time Phil had three trucks pulled over, three white drivers, two black co-drivers and two young boys. While all this was going on, the SAS were frantically working against time to lay all the charges. Grahame was not amused. All of a sudden he had a whole group of prisoners he had not bargained for. He could not leave them behind to tell the tale as to who had been responsible. Unlike the movies, he could not dispose of them. They would have to come with them but Combined Operations Headquarters (ComOps) in Rhodesia was not going to be at all happy. He ordered the fertilizer bags to be dumped, except those on the outside of the truck, and when all was ready, the SAS, prisoners, boats, canoes and equipment were loaded inside. The back of the truck was a perfect hideaway with all-round protection.

One of the captured brothers, who insisted on driving, climbed up into the cab as did Grahame with a silenced pistol. One can only imagine what the drivers were thinking. At 1225 hours the charges were initiated and the truck moved rapidly south, stopping some distance from the bridge as two men busied themselves cutting telephone wires. Just as they finished their job there was an almighty flash and they all felt the blast of detonation. The SAS knew that they had achieved their mission and would have given anything to see the effect of their intense efforts of the preceding days. They were joyous as they sped towards Mpika town. It was a likely trouble spot but the driver guided them around the bypass road. As daylight came, they turned off the main highway onto a dirt road leading into Luangwa Valley national park and south towards to the Rhodesian border. Grahame ordered a halt. The Rhodesian air force had dispatched a Canberra to the bridges at first light to assess the damage. Using the HF radio, Paul established communications with the forward listening station at Kariba, which flashed back the code word for 100 per cent success. They now knew that the mission had been a great success. The bridges were destroyed. It only remained to get everyone out. They pressed on but their route took them past relatively heavily populated areas, fortunately without incident. By this time the whole country must have been on the alert. The driver was most unhappy as was being forced to make his own route through the bush, over rocks and knocking down trees. The going was very rough and by late afternoon they could go no farther.

However, they were now within helicopter range of Rhodesia. Communications were established and they were told to prepare for pick-up the next morning. An LZ was prepared before they were finally able to fall into an exhausted sleep. Sentries kept watch through an uneventful night. The Zambians were searching in vain.

The next morning they cleared the last few trees in the LZ using the truck, much to the driver's dismay. The Bells had already begun their long, dangerous journey north into Zambia. They flew from Salisbury, refuelled at Mount Darwin then again at Musengezi mission, before crossing the border into Zambia. The helicopters carried fuel drums on board and using a simple but ingenious system, were able to refuel while in flight. As the fuel drums emptied they were jettisoned in flight.

As they neared the soldiers, Major Wilson, at the prearranged time, put out a continuous transmission on his VHF voice radio. The lead pilot homed in on it and the Bell helicopters touched down on the LZ. The SAS, prisoners and equipment were rapidly loaded up while the helicopter techs carried out a final

Chambeshi rail bridge after the operation. Photo *Rhodesia Herald*

refuel. Within fifteen minutes they were airborne and on their way for the long flight home, across Zambia and across the Cabora Bassa dam. The flight gave the men time to contemplate their spectacular achievement. On 13 October they touched down on Rhodesian soil.

For ten days Grahame and his free-fall team had been deeper inside enemy territory than any other Rhodesians before or since. They were faced with obstacles from the very onset, but undeterred, in the most professional and dedicated manner they carried out the reconnaissance. Captain Bob Mackenzie and his well-rehearsed and equally determined team joined them and together they overcame all the challenges to complete their mission with total success. Both bridges were destroyed and the full team was recovered to base without loss of life or injury. They returned with all of their very precious equipment which they could ill afford to lose. The Zambian economy was badly hurt and President Kenneth Kaunda found himself forced into a situation that suited Rhodesia and South Africa. Of all the external operations that I took part in, this was certainly the most varied, interesting and challenging. I was very proud to have been a small part of it. The prisoners were of course concerned about their fate right up the time they emplaned for the journey back to Zambia. No doubt they feared the worst from their ferocious-looking captors. The boys were the exception and enjoyed every minute of the adventure. They were well cared for in Rhodesia before finally being returned safely to Zambia.

8

Operation Tepid, October 1979

In October 1979, C Squadron was tasked with a reconnaissance mission in Zambia to search an area approximately forty-five kilometres north of Kariba town for a ZIPRA battalion thought to be in a defensive position with heavy weapons. This op was called Operation Tepid. Joshua Nkomo's ZIPRA was supported by the Soviets and was trained in classical warfare. ZIPRA did have some guerrilla units on the ground in Rhodesia, mainly in Matabeleland, but most of their troops were located in Zambia where they were known to be training for a conventional invasion of Rhodesia, probably in the Kariba area. It was suspected that ZIPRA might invade Kariba, seize the airfield and establish a government there. The Soviets could then recognize this government and fly in reinforcements which ostensibly might include Soviet, or more likely Cuban, ground forces, which might prove difficult to dislodge. The Cuban military were operating in Angola against the South Africans at this time and so the threat was taken seriously.

Earlier, a Rhodesian air force light aircraft flying low over Zambia north of Kariba had taken ground fire. A subsequent air reconnaissance by a photographic Canberra bomber then discovered a network of camouflaged trenches with footpaths leading between them. It was estimated that an enemy force up to battalion strength was entrenched here, possibly in preparation for an invasion of Kariba.

Two call signs of sixteen men each were formed to search the area. I was in call sign 31, the other call sign being 32. Our headquarters, call sign 30, was based at Kariba airfield. The leader of 31 was Phil 'Maggot' Cook, a lieutenant from New Zealand. Also in the call sign was Andy Anderson, ex-22 SAS. Five foreigners were attached to us from A Squadron. The remainder were all Rhodesian. After arriving at Kariba by truck from Salisbury, we established a tented camp and got our kit ready. I was the signaller and packed a TR48 HF radio and spare battery for long-distance Morse code communications, my personal VHF radio and spare batteries for voice communications, five days' water, ten days' rations, ammunition, grenades, sleeping gear, personal medical kit including saline drip, giving set, canula, claymore anti-personnel mine and an FN rifle.

Our call sign was inserted by two Bell Huey helicopters in an area of bush near the eastern side of the position in Zambia located by air the reconnaissance. On insertion, we walked towards a dirt road to search for spoor. The road had some old very spoor, all boot prints, but no vehicle spoor. I sent a situation report to call sign 30 informing them of our location and the spoor on the road. We immediately received a reply telling us to go into an ambush position on the road and await further instructions. We did this and waited for things to happen.

We deployed into a classical road-ambush situation. There were two end stops, each of four men, located up and down the road to give warning of anything approaching, with a killer group of eight men between the end stops. I was in the killer group with 'Maggot'. Claymore anti-personnel mines were sited and automatic weapons were allocated overlapping arcs of fire into the killing zone. We all worked in pairs, with each pair having one FN rifle and one belt-fed RPD machine gun. It was not the best of positions to ambush from but in the Zambezi valley it was about as good as it gets and we had plenty of firepower. It was stinking hot as it always is in the valley and dry as a bone.

After about an hour, one of the stop groups, call sign 31 Alpha, all A Squadron men, radioed to say that there was a group of approximately ten uniformed ZIPRA in extended line searching the road for spoor. These fellows knew what they were doing and were doing it properly. Then we heard shooting from the direction of 31A. They had been 'bumped' by the enemy. 31A called in on the 'small means', the VHF radio, to say they were withdrawing to our position and to expect them to enter our location in minutes.

31 Alpha arrived and so did ZIPRA. They weren't expecting a hot reception but they got one and withdrew immediately. We also withdrew to a new LUP in case they came back with some friends. I got off another report from our new position and was told to close down for one hour and await orders.

After an hour, we received our new orders: we were to move off to a new location and rendezvous with call sign 32 at first light the following morning. It was almost dark by that time and the distance involved, coupled with the thick bush, meant that this would be an all-night march. In the thick bush of the Zambezi valley a night march is not a pleasant walk, especially if the moon does not rise until the early hours of the morning. The area was thick with *wag 'n bietjie*, or 'wait a little bit', bush that has large, sharp thorns which point backwards and tear brutally into flesh and clothing alike. This stuff is a nightmare to walk through.

We set off at last light and Maggot set a cracking pace. After a couple of hours, one of our younger people, a slim, ginger-haired, pale-skinned fellow, went down with heat fatigue. He was in a bad way and was flushed with hot dry skin. The only thing to do was get some liquid down him, set up an intravenous drip and leave him behind with a couple of men to look after him. He might easily have died under these conditions if he had continued walking. Three men stayed with the casualty. They assisted him to the top of a nearby hill where they could hold off an attack if the bad guys came after them. The rest of the patrol, now numbering twelve, set off again.

At about 1100 hours our lead scout walked, by chance, over a sleeping body. There were muffled grunts in Sindebele which proved the sleeper was a Matabele and that we had stumbled upon ZIPRA. Then the shooting started. It was short and intense. The party with the heat-fatigue casualty was watching the tracers from their feature and said it was "like World War Three". There was green communist tracer and our red tracer all over the place. The dust next to me was being kicked up by incoming fire.

And then I saw stars and my head hurt badly. It felt as if I had been kicked in the head. I don't remember much, except that after being out cold for some seconds there was a very loud bang behind me and my shoulders and the back of my head hurt. I put my hand on the back of my head and it felt was warm and slippery as did the right side of my head. From behind me Maggot was shouting, "John's down. Are you alright?"

"No, I've been hurt as well," I replied.

Maggot told me and my buddy to pull back to his position. By now the shooting had stopped, so we stood up and ran back to his position behind a large anthill. John was on the ground with our medic, Roger, next to him. He had his medical kit out as he went through his immediate actions and underneath a poncho, examined the casualty by penlight torch. He called for assistance in holding up the poncho so he could do his vital job, whilst the rest of us went into all-round defence in case the enemy returned with reinforcements. Maggot got on the small means, his VHF radio, to the call sign with the heat-fatigue casualty to keep them informed. He then gave me a message to send to call sign 30 at Kariba to update them. I got the HF radio set up and after getting under another poncho with a penlight torch, had excellent communications immediately. Somebody was looking after us.

Strangely enough, I didn't feel too bad at this stage. I gave call sign 30 the book numbers, or code numbers, of the wounded personnel (John and me), requested immediate casevac for John and gave our location coordinates. The communications were excellent and I had no trouble in passing the message.

We were using a patrol code which had prearranged words and phrases suitable for all occasions, including this one, and it made encryption very quick and simple. It was also very secure because there were only two copies: I had one and call sign 30 the other.

Shortly after this my left arm became stiff and began to hurt like mad and my head hurt like buggery. Luckily Maggot permitted a fifty per cent alert, which meant one man out of each buddy pair could try to get some sleep.

Roger had got a saline drip into John but to no avail. He'd been hit badly and despite Roger's best efforts, he didn't make it.

First light was at 0500 and we immediately did a 360-degree clearance patrol of the area. The troops brought in the enemy kit that had been discarded, including grenades, a 3.5-inch rocket launcher, plenty of webbing and some rucksacks. Blood spoor and other signs indicated that three or four badly wounded or dead had been dragged off by a group of between eight and twelve enemy.

The Bell Huey helicopter arrived at about 0630 and John's body was loaded onto it. My arm was completely stiff by now and I could not put my rucksack on my back, so I got on the chopper as well. I would have been a liability in a contact. In the movies, when the hero gets a bullet wound in the head he wraps a bandage around his head and soldiers on. In real life it isn't like that. My head felt like it had been hit by a cricket bat, my vision was blurred and my head throbbed terribly. Delayed concussion was setting in.

Later that morning call sign 31 rendezvoused with call sign 32 and discovered the ZIPRA battalion entrenched on a high feature with several spurs. They located the enemy by advancing uphill along a spur when they came under fire from heavy weapons, probably Goryunovs, belt fed heavy machine guns firing rifle calibre bullets, and DShKs, belt fed heavy machine guns firing 12.7 mm ammunition, in trenches that later were found to have overlapping arcs of fire and overhead cover. The trenches were well sited and camouflaged, which was very likely the work of Soviet advisers. Maggot received a buttock wound and later received plenty of remarks such as "That's a bit of a bummer".

Call signs 31 and 32 were pulled out that evening in preparation for an attack the next day. Trucks were arriving at Kariba airfield in convoys from

Salisbury carrying the whole of the Rhodesian Light Infantry, including their cooks and clerks, and the entire SAS. There were probably 400 combat soldiers assembled. By Rhodesian standards this was going to be a major attack. The air force had summoned up nearly every jet aircraft and helicopter they could find. This operation was shaping up to become one of the biggest operations the Rhodesians had ever mounted. It was well and quickly organized with troops deployed into contact in twenty-four hours, a remarkable achievement.

The eleven Bell Huey helicopters choppered in approximately 400 men with a full-strength mortar platoon of eight tubes and ammunition and were to keep them well resupplied. Given the large area that ZIPRA troops occupied, the assault force was far too small in number and could not effectively seal off the entire perimeter. Assaults were made uphill by the Rhodesian ground troops against ZIPRA troops in trenches. The air force made numerous attacks with locally made napalm and fragmentation bombs. The Rhodesians suffered two men killed and several wounded.

Operation Tepid lasted for two days and three nights. ZIPRA, now estimated to be in company and not battalion strength, marched out through the perimeter with all their heavy weapons on the third night. An RLI call sign commander, a young subaltern, made the decision not to engage as they marched past his position. His men were the cooks, clerks and base personnel and had been the only troops left in camp at Kariba when his call sign was hastily cobbled together. Personally, I do not blame him for not opening fire as his group would likely have been overrun and annihilated. I believe an SAS call sign would have opened fire but one cannot compare a group of trained SAS soldiers with cooks, clerks, storemen and drivers who had been hurriedly deployed. Some senior officers were later overheard criticizing the young RLI subaltern but I do not believe the criticism was justified. It is one thing to criticize from the safety of a base camp but quite another to deploy into combat with a bunch of cooks and bottle-washers.

The Rhodesian security forces just did not have enough sufficiently trained infantry to secure the perimeter. In fact, they never ever had enough trained men.

9
The Cisco and Marianne Guerreiro story

I first met Cisco in the Rhodesian SAS when I signed on as a recruit in 1974. At that time he had re-enlisted in the SAS after completing a contract in the 1960s. He was married to Marianne. They were an unlikely couple but opposites appear to attract. Cisco was a man's man. Good with his hands he could make anything out of wood, throw concrete or build walls, while Marianne was a thinker who could communicate fluently in several languages and was a problem-solver. Often Marianne would come to the troopies' pub at Cranborne Barracks looking for Cisco who liked a drink now and again and again ... Marianne rose to become a lieutenant-colonel while Cisco was busted from sergeant to the ranks on numerous occasions. She was at her best controlling electronic 'eavesdropping' operations while he worked best with irregular indigenous troops on combat ops. Opposites attract. Cisco knew

Cisco and Marianne at home. 2007.

Ron Reid-Daly in the 1960s when Reid-Daly was the Regimental Sergeant-Major, or senior NCO, of the Rhodesian Light Infantry before he became Commanding Officer the Selous Scouts. Ron remembered Cisco and used his unique skills on several occasions. Cisco and Marianne are a unique couple with a unique story to tell. Here is their story in their own words.

Cisco's story

I left Portugal in 1948 when my family immigrated to Mozambique. We moved to Rhodesia in 1953. I was a plasterer's apprentice and when I was seventeen I went to Northern Rhodesia where I earned £60 to £75 a week which was big money in those days, but I spent it all. Once I hitchhiked to the Congo border and made it all the way to Nova Texeira in Angola. I returned to Rhodesia on a wood-burning train. All of this when I was seventeen.

I joined the Rhodesian SAS, C Squadron 22 SAS Regiment in January 1965. When Ian Smith declared UDI in November of that year we became C Squadron (Rhodesian) SAS. I was on guard duty at Kariba dam when UDI was declared. We were there a month, four hours on and four hours off. We had machine-gun emplacements and so on. I was cleaning my rifle when that little guy who eventually became the boss—he was a lieutenant then— made me a lance-corporal. That was for chasing those guys who killed the Viljoen family in Karoi area all the way up to Sipolilo and beyond; they were finally killed by the Portuguese commandos in Mozambique. I got my first stripe for outstanding something or other on a Friday and decided to celebrate. I went to town on Saturday and met Costa Polentes's friend at the Park Lane hotel. We met two sisters and that was the end of the weekend because I remember nothing after that. I was supposed to be guard commander on Sunday but I never pitched. So I was demoted on Monday by the little guy and after that we never saw eye to eye. He was jumping up and down, saying, "Are you trying to make me look like Jimmy the C**t?" and the redder he got the more I laughed. That was the first time I went absent. So I was lance-corporal for three days and got confined to barracks for seven. Which was a record!

I left the army the first time when I bought myself out for the last year for £25. I went back to plastering. In 1971 I went back to Mozambique where I joined the volunteers on the outskirts of Gorongosa national park. I did that for two years. Then I went to Cabora Bassa dam until 1974. In January 1974, when Frelimo took over Mozambique, I went back to Rhodesia. I rejoined the SAS. I had to do another selection course. I made full corporal. However, I

Cisco in the SAS, the first time. *Photo* Cisco Guerreiro

went AWOL again at the School of Infantry in 1975. So it was back to troopie again, which was par for the course.

In 1976 the adjutant of SAS came to pick me up when I was guard commander and told me to pack up all my kit and go to the Selous Scouts. So the Scouts guys picked me up and took me to Inkomo barracks. This was a very quick and unexpected move a few days before the Scouts attack on Nyadzonya camp in Mozambique. Ron Reid-Daly put me in the front truck of the column, dressed as a Frelimo political commissar. One night we crossed the border in a long column. Paul Holt was driving an armoured car and put it into a ditch [see Marianne's story following]. He got onto our truck and we laid up near the town of Vila Manica. There is a road that goes to Tete and we took it. Captain Warraker, who was in charge of the column, made us lay up until early morning when the terrorists got on parade at eleven o'clock. We had eighty one men in our column. The terrorists reportedly numbered 1,200.

We drove into the camp and stopped in a line. I started speaking to the terrorists. I said in Portuguese through a loudhailer "*Camaradas*, we have learned that there are traitors to our cause here. We are looking for traitors.

Come here. Will your leaders come forward? *Camaradas. Nos estamos aqui para averiguar certos assuntos. Temos conhecimento que se encontram traidores a nossa causa aqui. Portanto os vossos chefes venham ate aqui para discutirmos estes assuntos.* Comrades, we are here to tell you certain things. We want you to know that we all have the same cause. Our chiefs come to discuss certain things." I delivered this in a local accent.

They ran towards us, shouting and cheering until one terrorist saw one of our men with blue eyes. We were all disguised with 'black is beautiful' camo cream. He stopped and pointed at Blue Eyes and started shouting: "*Murungu!*" which means white man in Shona. Captain Warraker then shouted "Fire!" and we opened up. We had two, I think, 20mm cannons, many MAG machine guns and AK rifles. It was all over in fifteen minutes. We had one man shot through both legs but that was all. We killed most of the enemy.

There was, however, a man shooting at us from a two-metre-high bank. Captain Warraker said, "Go get him, Cisco." When I got there he was dead. They had shot him over our heads. Then we went into the buildings and huts looking for papers and so on and then set fire to the buildings. I was with Paul Holt. We heard the trucks moving out and he turned to me and said, "They can't be leaving without us."

I said, "I got news for you, pal; they've f***ed off and left us."

A little later we heard the *boom* as the column blew the bridge on their way out.

Paul and I each had about thirty-seven rifle rounds left and it took us three days to get back to Rhodesia. We walked along the Pungwe river to the Katiya Tea Estate and up to Inyanga. All we had to eat was three limes from a lime tree we came across. We followed a game track and crossed the Pungwe from rock to rock where the locals had placed tree trunks for a ford. As we crossed the river on the last night, which was the third day, I threw the logs into the water so it would be difficult for the pursuers to follow us.

When we got to the other side, Paul wanted a fire. I said "Are you crazy? Let's cross this kopje and then we'll camp for the rest of the night."

But he wouldn't move. He said, "A man can only take so much." He really wanted a fire very badly. I suppose he was still whoozy from the accident and not used to going on his own two feet. We were only fifty yards across and anyone following could have shot us. I was so mad at the time that I even considered leaving him but couldn't. So I made a small fire and shielded it with a *boma* of palm leaves, checking afterwards to see if there was any chink of light showing.

Paul collapsed by the fire and lay dozing, opening his eyes every now and then looking at me. At one stage, he said, "Christ, you old bastard, don't you ever sleep?"

I said "Not till you and me are safe, pal."

Next morning we set off and crossed the Pungwe border through knee-high water. I had been checking the line of the Inyanga mountains. This was when we bumped into a stick of police reservists on border duty who were moving out with a new team coming in. They were all very nervous of us with their fingers on their triggers.

We had taken off our green shirts and wrapped our AKs in them so they could see we were white. The first thing we did was get a beer. The team we were with couldn't get comms, so they took us in their truck into the mountains where Special Branch had a comms unit. While we were in the truck with the spotter planes overhead looking for us, Paul activated his strobe light. The SB commander snatched it away and put it in his pocket, saying, "What's that?"

Taking the mickey, I said, "You don't know what you've just done. What you've just put in your pocket, pal. When he pressed the button to arm it, he activated a small bomb which is due to go off in a few seconds."

The commander made a grab for it then relaxed. "You guys and your f***ing gadgets."

There were two Special Branch guys at the camp who immediately took us to a tent and gave us *ganga* overalls to wear. The police reservists were told not to speak to us and to go on their way. The funny thing was that while we were in the truck, I recognized Mr Lord who was the father of my daughter's best friend at school and after a while he said, "I know you."

I said, "So you should. I was at your house playing darts last Sunday after lunch." This helped the police commander to accept us, as he had been very nervous and suspicious of the two weird *ouens*.

Special Forces then called up a chopper and within twenty minutes we were picked up and on our way to New Sarum where we were taken by vehicle back to camp. They were all waiting for us at the Scouts all-ranks pub; there was Ian Smith, Ron Reid-Daly and lots of big knobs. Ian Smith shook my hand and said, "Well done, my boy."

I went AWOL once again. I borrowed Reid-Daly's Land Rover and disappeared for two weeks. This time I got twenty-eight days' detention. When I returned to the SAS, the little man was now the boss.

Author with Cisco Guerreiro in his 'local', 2007.

I was then contacted by another Portuguese, Orlando Cristina, who came from Portimão in the Algarve, and another guy to go and join them in the Mozambique National Resistance (MNR). They said they needed me in the resistance but for that I would need to be kicked out of the army. That's when I went AWOL again and got another twenty-eight days' detention. And I got kicked out of the army.

I was the most 'AWOLest' person in the army.

I was talking to Len Monson who was in charge of the RLI gym when someone from the Prime Minister's Office came in and said his boss was outside and wanted to talk to me. So I went outside and chatted. He said, "Would you like to come and work with us?" He wanted me to go and work at the camp at Udzi in the eastern districts. That was 22 June 1977, which I remember because it was the day before my birthday. A few days later I went to Udzi. At that time there were twenty-five MNR and when I left there were about six hundred. Andrea Matsangaise was the chief of the MNR at that time. He was killed near Gorongosa in 1979, I think in a contact with Frelimo. We all had a lot of trouble with Andrea.

After Rhodesia I joined 5 Recce as a staff sergeant. While with them I went on the Maputo raid in a similar role as in the Selous Scouts raid as well as working under cover. I had three passports, Portuguese, South African and

Swazi, all in different names. Sometimes I got confused. Who am I today? What name am I using? I was with 5 Recce for five years.

After I left the SADF, it was back to building. We returned to Portugal in 1993 after the death of my parents and I inherited my grandfather's house from my mother.

And here we are, sitting in the sun at the local pub drinking a few well-earned *chibulis* [beers].

Marianne's story
I joined the Rhodesian army, the Rhodesian Women's Service (RWS), in 1975, the second intake. We had some fun times, especially on basic training when the RSM of the RLI, old Iron Jaw himself [Harry Springer] gave us handbag drill He looked most amusing with a handbag instead of his pace stick.

I was posted to R Troop, the eavesdropping troop. The South Africans were there at that time and we had just begun to look at Mozambique and Angola as well as Zambia and Botswana, and to recruit a lot of Portuguese-speakers,

Marianne Guerreiro with her Rhodesian Signals Corps troop, 1976. *Photo* Marianne Guerreiro

both regulars and national service. This was a whole new ball game as the communications used were no longer based on NATO but were on the systems used by the Russians and the Cubans. I had to learn Morse code, and naturally my English, Afrikaans and Portuguese came in very handy, particularly for translating the finished product. I later learned Russian and can still read the Cyrillic alphabet to this day.

Our regular members, both male and female, picked up the Russian communications system very quickly, and could decrypt the voice codes into plain language almost as fast as it was being sent. As mentioned, I was doing the translating and got interested in analyzing the systems used, the call signs, the codes etc., which varied with the different units involved and this began our signals intelligence.

No one took our signals intercepts very seriously at the time and the attitude of the 'ops bods' was let's see what the enemy was saying only while we beat them up. However, the Intelligence Corps, Military Intelligence and others began to see the possibilities and we were expanded into 8 Signals Squadron with radio direction finding and other sophisticated equipment. Our intercept capability became so good and the signals intelligence team improved so much that we could give the ops personnel a complete order of battle (ORBAT) of the areas they were interested in. People began to take us very seriously and things at 8 Squadron changed dramatically. We became involved in most cross-border ops with small units attached to the Int personnel at forward HQs for close support during the ops.

There were many amusing incidents during this time, one of which was the famous 'Green Leader' intercept and recording of the inbound aircraft and the Lusaka tower during the attack on the ZIPRA camp, Westlands Farm, outside Lusaka in late 1978.

Pilot: "Just who is in charge here?"

Tower: "Well, I think the Rhodesians are."

We all had a good laugh at that.

I remember doing the back-up for the attack on the Nyadzonya camp. With 'need to know', I was not aware that Cisco was on the ground there and only much later did Ron Reid-Daly tell me that after four days' missing in action, he was wondering how to tell me that Cisco was not back. We intercepted the messages confirming Paul Holt's accident with the armoured car, the attack and the bridge being blown.

It was very strange working in the electronic-collection business as we had

Marianne receives the Southern Cross medal from General Viljoen, 1985. *Photo* Marianne Guerreiro

Marianne Guerreiro with her South African uniform and medals, 2007.

THE CISCO AND MARIANNE GUERREIRO STORY 155

a completely different view of the situation, mostly from the enemy point of view.

I ended up as a captain in Rhodesia and after Cisco went south in 1980, I followed suit. After six months in civilian life, I joined the SADF and was posted to Chief of Staff Intelligence instead of Signals. I retired as a lieutenant-colonel in 1993. I worked with the army, air force and navy in electronic warfare proper. Our electronic communications units were mobile and roved the battlefields with the troops on the front line.

I remember when the South Africans captured a SAM-6 rocket battery complete with operator and rockets. The attack on their brigade had been very heavy and the SAAF was preventing the Cubans from giving them air support. This resulted in the brigade being pulled back. Our operator heard the SAM-6 commander telling his brigade commander that he could not move as he had no fuel. The message was in code but our SIGINT section had a very smart, young female Portuguese corporal, Maria de Jesús, who broke the code. She later married one of the Chilean pilots attached to us and who was monitoring the Cuban air force. This decrypt gave us the gist of the message as well as a six-figure grid reference which was promptly passed on to the Special Forces units at the front. The next thing we knew was that the SAM-6 battery was in Grootfontein, South West Africa, on its way back to Pretoria.

My SIGINT section were all awarded the Chief of Staff Army Defence Medal (CSADF) and I received the Southern Cross Medal (SM).

I believe that despite sanctions, the Americans and the Israelis were onto this in a flash as it was the first working SAM-6 to fall into western hands. At that time their air forces were training against SAM-6 mock-ups. We later used this same SAM-6 to train our radar and intercept operators.

With our forward-intercept and radio-direction-finding units working inside enemy territory, it was inevitable that we should also suffer casualties. We had casualties in Angola when a Cuban bomb fell into a foxhole and we had several killed. In Mozambique the weather was to blame when the unit was on a hilltop and lightning struck an antenna and then skipped across to a tent pole and onto a camp bed killing a young signaller.

Just before retiring I had my own department of twenty people within the Electronic Collection (EC) HQ, mainly linguists and analysts. The code-breakers worked in a separate department and were seconded to us for ops.

10
Mozambique National Resistance

The Mozambique National Resistance had its origins, so I was told by a Portuguese who worked for them, in 1974, just after Frelimo took control of Mozambique. In April 1974 there had been a socialist revolution in Portugal which brought to power a government that had no interest in colonies that were a financial and military burden. The new socialist regime decided to get rid of Guinea Bissau, Mozambique and East Timor but attempted to retain Angola due to the oil reserves in the province of Cabinda. With Mozambique controlled by the Portuguese, Rhodesia had a secure port, a secure pipeline for oil imports, sanctions-busting offices and a gateway to the world. When Mozambique was given independence all this was lost and Rhodesia became increasingly dependent on South Africa. A Portuguese government delegation arrived in Mozambique in April 1974 with the message that independence would be granted to the colony the following October. All Portuguese citizens would be assisted, if they wished, to return to Portugal. They could only take one suitcase each. As you can imagine, a message like that created panic amongst much of the Portuguese population and large numbers fled to South Africa and Rhodesia. The rest packed their suitcases and waited at Beira and Lourenço Marques (later Maputo) airports for the fleet of Boeing 707s to arrive and ferry them back to Lisbon. After 500 years of Portuguese occupation, the whole country virtually folded up overnight.

Frelimo was only one of several liberation movements in Mozambique and this was the one chosen by the Portuguese to take over the reins of power. Actually, it was more a case of "We're pulling out now and if you want the place, you can have it." No Portuguese stayed on in the former colony and there were no plans to train any future adminstrators, tax collectors, soldiers, doctors, technicians and so on. Frelimo inherited a bankrupt country with no tax base, no mineral wealth of any kind and little prospect of any hope for the future. The country was ripe for the Soviet Union to provide 'assistance'.

A small number of Portuguese ex-soldiers formed 'The Movement' to oppose the new Frelimo government. They were badly organized, poorly armed and after several brushes with the new Frelimo army, FPLM, moved to

Andrea Matsangaise. *Photo* Cisco Guerreiro

Rhodesia to look for help. One of the Mozambicans to look to Rhodesia for aid in fighting Frelimo was Andrea Matsangaise. He once owned a bulldozer and a Mercedes motorcar after making a lot of money during construction work on Cabora Bassa dam. However, the new Frelimo government took away both his car and his bulldozer, which was why he joined The Movement. However, he was generally considered to be very difficult to deal with. In Rhodesia, Special Branch 'B' under Mr Mac took The Movement in hand and established a base for them in the northeast of Rhodesia near Nyamapanda. The base was situated on an abandoned farm close to the border. At first, I don't think anybody knew exactly what to do with these people. However, it must have been felt that they might be useful at a later date to help secure Rhodesia's eastern border. The British South Africa Police (BSAP) ran the show entirely on their own at this stage with some Portuguese personnel from the Rhodesian army, The Movement and one retired army officer.

Initially, the MNR organization was slow to take off. Recruiting drives in Mozambique were carried out and at first had little success. However, the Frelimo regime quickly became unpopular and recruitment into the MNR improved. Frelimo press-ganged young men into the army and forced farmers

Frelimo soldiers pose for the camera before going on operations. *Photo* author's collection

off their land and into collective farms. These and further unpopular measures, combined with a sense of disillusionment at the direction the country was taking, played into the hands of the MNR.

By 1977, it was decided that the MNR had the ability, with the right management and organization, to secure the eastern border of Rhodesia. That same year the camp at Nyamapanda was attacked by FPLM and effectively put out of operation. Frelimo clearly understood that the MNR was a danger to their regime and decided to destroy it. The MNR training camp was then moved to an abandoned tobacco farm at Udzi near the town of Umtali in the Manicaland province.

In 1978 the BSAP handed over the training and operation of MNR to the Rhodesian SAS. I came into the picture in early 1979 when I first visited the camp at Udzi. The MNR recruits were housed in the old tobacco barns while the Portuguese instructors lived in what was once the farmhouse. This 'team house' that the instructors lived in was protected by trenches and had a mortar pit for an 81mm mortar in the garden. The barns were ringed with

 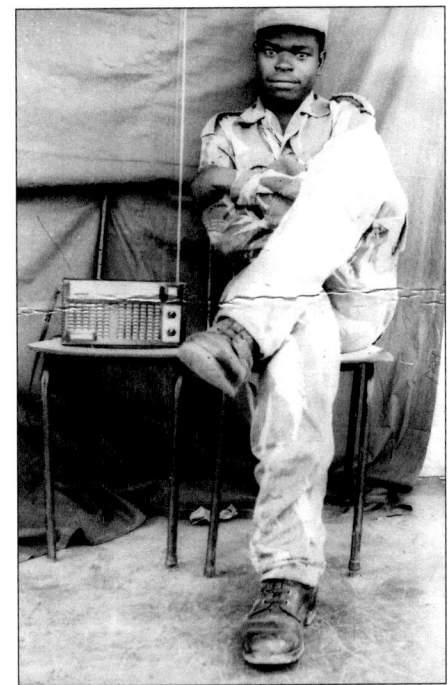

Frelimo soldiers

trenches and bunkers that provided defence in depth. The camp could have withstood a determined attack from FPLM. An army major, Dudley Coventry, was in overall command. He had once been OC C Squadron SAS and had Second World War experience as an army commando, seeing action during the Normandy campaign. Unfortunately, he was killed by an 'intruder' at his house in Zimbabwe in the 1980s.

Training of the MNR was run by a Portuguese called Cristina. Unfortunately, he was killed by an 'intruder' in his apartment in Johannesburg in the 1980s. Coincidence?

In mid-1979 it was decided to send two columns of MNR into central-southern Mozambique to establish firm operating bases with advisers from the SAS. One column, commanded by Andrea with Lieutenant F and three operators as advisers, went to the Gorongosa area in central Mozambique near Beira. This is a 3,500-feet-high plateau with sub-tropical foliage, a higher-than-average rainfall and among other things, wild cattle. Under the Portuguese it had been a national park. The column crossed the border on foot and marched to the plateau where they established a base. At the end of this first operation, we were told that Andrea had been killed in a fight with Frelimo. A force of

Frelimo soldiers

Frelimo had arrived at the base of the plateau with T-34 tanks and infantry with the aim of destroying the MNR group. Andrea decided to make a frontal assault on the enemy and was killed leading his men in a charge across open ground. He was then replaced by his 2 i/c, Afonso Dlakahma.

The other column, which comprised 350 MNR men, was led by Luke Mhlanga, a tall, slim African who had been born just inside Rhodesia on the border with Mozambique. I had worked with Luke several times before in eastern districts when we crossed the border into Mozambique to meet contact men or set ambushes. The Rhodesian and Mozambican international boundaries were marked only by a wire fence which means little to African villagers who cross borders frequently to trade and marry. Luke had been an officer with Frelimo and had been trained by the Soviets, but he later became disillusioned with the Frelimo organization.

Another column of approximately 150 MNR entered Mozambique to the north of Espungabera in southern Gaza province with four SAS advisers. After only three days, the sergeant in charge of the SAS, van B, and one operator went down with severe diarrhoea. The two remaining operators, Andy and Harry, were still fit. These two were both farm boys 'in tune' with the bush

Luke Mhlanga with captured Chinese 82mm mortar, 1979.

and as we used to say, 'bush fit'. I and a very young, fair-haired recent arrival to C Squadron were tasked to replace van B and the other casualty. During our briefing from the OC at SAS, we were told that we would fly to the MNR camp by helicopter and van B would carry out a handover before he and the other guy left on the same chopper. It was intended we should recruit more people for the group then move south to Espungabera, which we should capture. Resupplies would then be trucked in by road into Espungabera for the MNR.

It all sounded very easy.

When my companion and I arrived at the MNR camp, known as 'Charlie 5', by Alouette III helicopter, we got off the chopper and walked across to the whites I could see in the tree line at the edge of the clearing. Van B rushed across to the chopper, threw a medical pack at me and climbed on board. He didn't even say hello. I was very disappointed as this showed a complete lack of professionalism and a breakdown in personal discipline. This man was later disappointing in other ways in both his military and civilian career. Luckily, the remaining operators were both fine and after seeing Luke Mhlanga, with whom I had a long chat about old times, we got a brew going and discussed the current situation. Andy and Harry called Luke Mhlanga 'Luke the Gook' and the name stuck. Harry was our signaller. He soon had the HF radio in operation and we sent a coded message to SAS HQ in Salisbury informing them of our safe arrival.

The group was divided into four 'commands': Luke was overall commander and had his own headquarters command comprising signaller, medical orderly, a mortar group of four 60mm mortar tubes with base plates and bipods and his bodyguards; The other three commands were purely infantry, each with a designated commander.

The MNR men were well equipped by African army standards. Each man was armed with an AMD assault rifle, made in Hungary and which was essentially a cut-down AK-47. They each had a green shirt and trousers, a green combat jacket and a green floppy hat. Webbing was Soviet-style AK chest webbing with a green web belt and pouches. Every man had a small rucksack for his personal kit and marched in black canvas boots with rubber soles.

Next day, the column set off. We moved in single file with the four white advisers at the rear. There were frequent stops as the column snaked towards the area of Gogoi where it was intended we set up our first firm base. It was

The team with Luke Mhangla and MNR commanders, 1979.

very hot and the flies were a distraction. On the march we began recruiting people. I estimate that after two days' march, we had 500 in our column when we reached a high feature near Gogoi. The local people were complaining about the Frelimo government and how their possessions were being stolen by the FPLM soldiers.

A few problems arose in the first week. The young, fair-haired, fair-skinned operator who had arrived with me developed diarrhoea. It got worse very quickly and after ten days in Mozambique, he became debilitated to the point where he was unable to walk. I was seriously concerned about his wellbeing. I wanted him evacuated quickly. I did not require a replacement for him as I thought we three survivors were a tight, well-knit team and we could cope adequately. We were all bush fit and comfortable with the situation.

The other problem concerned one of Luke's commanders, known as Benjamin. Informers told me that he was spreading rumours about Luke and it was clear he wanted to depose Luke and become the top man. This was a serious development as it might cause some disruption to the operation. I got Harry to encrypt a message to Salisbury asking for a helicopter casevac for our casualty and for the removal of Benjamin. I suggested a cover story for Benjamin's departure which was that he was wanted back at the Udzi base as a trainer for new recruits. Luke was in agreement regarding his removal. Harry tapped out the message in Morse code with Andy cranking the pedal generator to provide the electrical power. We received a reply next day. The casevac helicopter would be arriving that afternoon. Shortly afterwards, Luke received a message from his base ordering Benjamin to return to Udzi for recruit training duties. He was to depart on the same helicopter as the casualty.

Day by day recruits came into our camp and we were getting worried about our ability to feed them. I got Harry to send a message on one of our daily 'scheds', or radio schedules, indicating our need to equip and feed some 500 new recruits and feed our original 150 men.

We got a reply next day to stand by for resupply. This was unexpectedly quick. The day after this we had a message telling us that the resupply would be at our location that afternoon at 1600 hours by parachute. This was an unusually rapid response and an indication of the importance of the MNR operation.

No number of aircraft was mentioned, nor was any information given regarding the logistics we would receive. I anticipated a resupply of one, or perhaps two, DC-3 Dakota aircraft and maybe two or three tons of kit. We sorted out a drop zone and waited. At 1700 we heard the aircraft and contacted them on our small VHF radios. I threw smoke when they got close and guided them onto the area where we wanted the loads to land. I was amazed when I saw six DC-3s. I called them in one by one giving the "Go left … go right … roll out … steady … stand by the lights … red light on … green light on … go!" and we ended up with most of the loads in a tight area near the camp.

Then I had one of the biggest shocks of my life. From out of nowhere came a white C-130 at less than 300 feet above my head. Pallets came rolling out the back on multiple parachutes. I can't remember how many pallets arrived. I had never in my wildest dreams imagined we would get this kind of logistic support. The C-130 Hercules aircraft was painted white and the pilot spoke in an Afrikaans accent. It was clearly a SAFAIR aircraft owned by the South African government. SAFAIR at that time had the world's largest 'privately' owned C-130 fleet. I say non-military but they were the only 'civilian' C-130 planes I have ever seen with static lines for paratroopers and red and green jump lights. Unfortunately, the US government would not supply C-130s with strengthened floors so they were limited to one-ton pallets. This use of SAFAIR

MNR troops parade following air resupply, 1979.

aircraft was a clear statement that the MNR had a high priority in the South African government's view and morale in the MNR soared to new heights. Luke was very happy. Recruit training began in the commands with enough rifles to arm every recruit.

Another part of a recruit's life in the MNR was to listen to Luke giving *hombera* which entails talking to the ancestors and asking for their help and protection. Almost every African in sub-Saharan Africa is part Christian and part Animist. Africans like to cover all the angles regarding God and the afterlife. This way they can't lose. About once a week Luke would get several hundred MNR men together and would stand in front of them. The men would squat and slowly and quietly clap their hands. This is *hombera*. Meanwhile, Luke would talk loudly in a monotone voice and seemingly go into a trance. The sound of the slow, rhythmic clapping and Luke's monotone would induce an almost hypnotic state in the audience. After fifteen minutes or so, Luke would raise his voice and the clapping would become louder and quicker. With three loud claps from Luke the audience would wake from their dream state, stand up and disperse. It was an amazing thing to watch. The feeling in the place was very strange and one could almost taste the atmosphere. I sometimes think they really do communicate with their ancestors.

Bunkers were built in the camp and trenches were dug. Patrols were sent out into the countryside and Frelimo were engaged several times. Posto Gogoi, the government post and Gogoi Comercial, the business centre, were occupied by the MNR. A number of weapons was also captured. Luke was exceptionally keen to have them under his personal control. I later learned that he received a cash bonus for every ZANLA or FPLM weapon captured. The cash was supplied by Special Branch and given to his wife who lived at the camp at Udzi.

Electronic intelligence from the Rhodesian Corps of Signals indicated that Frelimo were sending a mobile battalion from Nova Sofala to attack us. A Frelimo mobile battalion was an infantry battalion mounted in Soviet BTR 152 six-wheeled armoured trucks. This posed a problem because we had only a limited anti-armour capability. We had a few RPG-7 rocket launchers but I had no faith in the ability of our rocketeers. It takes practice to make a good rocketeer.

The Rhodesian Air Force came to our rescue with some Hawker Hunter jet fighters. Several Frelimo vehicles in a column approached on a road to our north. The vehicles stopped and launched some 122mm rockets in our general direction. They were ineffective. We requested jet effort and the Hunters took

Captured Frelimo soldier in Luke's base camp, 1979.

Captured 82mm mortar in Luke Mhlanga's base camp, 1979.

out several vehicles. A few Frelimo were killed by the MNR and the Frelimo column turned tail and ran. The MNR marked out their territory in their usual way by cutting off the heads of the corpses and sticking them on poles in the road. One FPLM soldier was captured alive and was brought back to our camp. He was very frightened and thought he was due to meet his ancestors. Luke pardoned him and offered him a place in the MNR. This was a good piece of public relations. Once word got around that Frelimo fighters could desert and join the MNR, it would be easier to get them to desert.

After nine weeks with the MNR, we received a coded message that we were to expect uplift in the next few days. The next day, without warning, two Bell Huey helicopters arrived and landed on the LZ we had cleared close to our main base. These Huey aircraft had been bought from Israel as 'fully reconditioned' but were found to be in a poor state of maintenance when they arrived. Even so, they were a welcome addition to the ageing fleet of Alouette III aircraft. The Hueys provided a massive increase in load-carrying ability and a greater endurance than that of the Alouette.

The two helicopters shut down and Andy, Harry and I walked across to see who had arrived. We found out it was some SAS B Squadron men. They brought with them, what seemed to us to be huge amounts of tinned food and other goodies and appeared to be about to settle in for a comfortable and relaxing stay. We, on the other hand, had been reduced to drying out old teabags and bartering for 'marathon' chickens from the locals. We would trade two yards of coloured cotton cloth for one chicken. These chickens were so skinny they looked as if they had run a marathon, hence the name "marathon chickens". In Africa the best thing for bartering is cheap printed cotton because the women like to make dresses out of it.

Andy, Harry and I rapidly packed our kit. We had only one rucksack each, which was always kept packed and ready to move and jumped onto the chopper. The helicopter took us all the way back to Udzi, and put us down at the rear of the house at the MNR camp. Cristino came over to the aircraft and took us across to the house. He showed us our beds and told us that Major Coventry would be back shortly to debrief us. He gave us soap, towels, shorts and T-shirts. After that we had our first good meal in two months.

The major arrived soon afterwards and we had a long chat about the situation at the base, the state of the men and prominent personalities. I told him that the group were ready to start expanding and that they were in complete control of the area around the base. I told him Luke now had 1,250

Frelimo revolutionary poem.

Eu gostaria
       de ser capaz
de escrever um poema
que fosse tão belo, tão exaltante,
inspirador e profundo
como a vitória do povo.

Um poema que contasse
toda a luta, e a maneira
como o povo a fez
          e a venceu.

Um poema que ao ouvi-lo
alguém do povo dissesse:
"Assim foi. Tal lugar
eu conheço, foi a base onde lutei.
"Assisti a tal massacre,
perdi nele os meus dois filhos.
"Em tal batalha abatemos
três aviões portugueses.
"Nessa aldeia vivi: um traidor
trouxe um dia a repressão.
"Namatil? Conheço. Aí prendemos
uma unidade inimiga."

Um poema que lembrasse
os heróis sacrificados:
com os corpos construíram
a ponte
      necessária
que nos levou à vitória.

Um poema que explicasse
a razão porque vencemos:
era o povo que lutava –
o povo inteiro, guiado
por uma linha correcta.

Um poema que indicasse
            finalmente
o porquê da nossa luta:
a vida nova que estamos construindo,
a liberdade,
o orgulho de sermos quem nós somos,
a negação
     radical
da exploração.

         *
    *   *

Alguém um dia há-de escrever
isto que já é vida
antes de ser poema.

frelimo

men in the camp, most of who were armed. He seemed satisfied.

The next morning transport arrived to take us back to Salisbury where the whole of C Squadron was waiting to welcome us. They had been busy while we were away and had made one raid by chopper into Mozambique where they had dropped two bridges in addition to damaging other items of infrastructure. The military pressure was steadily being applied to the Frelimo government to persuade them to stop supporting terrorism.

The day after we arrived back at Kabrit barracks, my two colleagues, Andy and Harry and I were called into the office of the SAS 2 i/c for a debrief on our stay with Luke Mhlanga's group. Also in the room were three people from Special Branch that I didn't recognize. They all wore nicely tailored dark business suits, white shirts, dark ties, carried briefcases and were clean shaven with neat haircuts. They could have been taken for insurance salesmen. The 2 i/c ran the meeting and he cut me and my colleagues short if he thought we were saying too much or he didn't like what we were saying. My impression was that he wanted to control the meeting. One of the SB men asked me if we had spent enough time with the MNR. I replied that it was not a good thing to send teams in for only a few weeks at a time. This failed to produce any continuity of advice or training and the teams would not develop a rapport with the MNR. In addition, I suggested that this kind of work was best done by long-service senior NCOs rather than very young soldiers. I referred to my service with Selous Scouts. I was asked how long I would be prepared to go into the bush for. I said I would do three months with the MNR, but I would want a good cash bonus in my hand when I returned. He said this could be done. The SAS 2i/c quickly responded that "SAS don't take bonuses" but the body language of the SB guys indicated otherwise.

I asked around and there were three others in C Squadron who said they would do a three-month stint with me. Andy Anderson wanted to go and there were two Rhodesians. We got as far as drawing ninety days' compo rations for four men but we were never deployed. I was, however, to go on further ops with the MNR.

Relocating the Mozambique National Resistance

In March 1980, following the disastrous outcome of the one-man one-vote elections in Zimbabwe–Rhodesia (as the country was temporarily now named), it was clear that the MNR had to be moved out of Rhodesia. The new regime headed by Robert Mugabe was due to take control of the government in April.

A new home needed to be found for the MNR, and their current home at the farm in Udzi had to be cleared.

C Squadron SAS was tasked for an operation in the east of Rhodesia early in March. All operators in the squadron packed terrorist 'greens': green shirt and trousers and communist webbing with AK-47 rifles or RPD belt-fed machine guns, though we travelled to the area of operations in Rhodesian kit. The squadron, about forty men in a road convoy, left the camp early one morning and headed for the Melsetter area on the eastern border. The precise location and our mission were secrets known only to Captain MacKenzie, our American OC.

The following day we moved to a location on the border and established a camp. All vehicles were parked under trees and covered in camouflage. No trenches were dug but sleeping areas were sited to give all-round defence.

That night we were briefed on our mission, which was to send two men from the SAS with a patrol of South African Reconnaissance Commandos into Mozambique to locate the MNR group commanded by Luke Mhlanga. We were not informed what the SADF personnel wanted to see the MNR about. It appeared that there had been a breakdown in communications between Luke Mhlanga's group and the base in Rhodesia. The South Africans would be arriving by Puma helicopter in one or two days and the whole operation should be complete one week thereafter.

The SAS men detailed were me and Trooper J, a young man of Afrikaans origin. Trooper J was a South African and had previously served in the South African Parachute Battalions. He was extremely fit but very skinny and of medium height. He ate very little but still had a lot of stamina. He was a Comrades Marathon silver medallist, which means he could run ninety-two kilometres in under seven and a half hours, an impressive feat which I could not possibly match. My best time for that race was ten hours.

The following afternoon, two camouflaged Puma helicopters arrived from the south flying along the Rhodesian–Mozambican border. One helicopter landed and four men with kit climbed out. The helicopter took off and departed the way it had come in. The four South African soldiers, from 1 Recce Commando based in Durban, were all wearing a grey uniform of shirt and trousers and carried rucksacks. The difference between them and us was immediately apparent. They were dressed and armed identically, whereas we all had differences in dress and equipment. In the Rhodesian army one supplied or made most of one's own webbing equipment and we often carried

MOZAMBIQUE NATIONAL RESISTANCE

Author with 82mm mortar in MNR base camp, 1979.

captured equipment like pistols, holsters, webbing and so on. Our equipment was battered and scratched and scruffy but it all worked. By comparison, the South Africans were kitted out in identical new uniforms, identical new rifles, very nice new rucksacks and identical new personal webbing. They looked very smart and had the sheen of civilization upon them. We, however, looked as if we had lived in the bush for years, which we had.

We found a spot for the Recces to sleep and had a chat with them. Their leader was Captain Steyn who was Afrikaans. There was another younger Afrikaner, an English-speaking South African and a coloured chap, Anthony, from Angola. Captain Steyn and the other Afrikaner were very stand-offish and aloof. However, the English-speaking South African and the Angolan were very easy to get along with. The English-speaker was from Durban and was the medic in the patrol. The coloured guy was originally from Luanda and had been training to be a commercial artist before the Portuguese socialist revolution in April 1974. He then joined Holden Roberto's FNLA which was bankrolled by the American CIA and was involved in the fighting in Angola in 1975/76. He knew several of the Brit contract soldiers, including the notorious Costas 'Colonel Callan' Georgio who was one of the leaders of Roberto's contract force. Anthony told me he had watched Costas shoot several of the contract soldiers who had taken FNLA pay and then refused to fight when the going got tough. He said to me that Costas was perfectly justified in shooting the men since the group had their backs to the wall and he needed every man he could get. Their defence, he said, was starting to crumble and shooting the men stiffened the resolve of the remaining people. Such is the life of the contract soldier.

Next morning Trooper J, the four Recces and I jumped in one of the trucks and were taken up to the border fence. We crossed over into Mozambique just before dawn and Steyn set a cracking pace up a river valley. It was apparent Steyn did not know the exact location of the MNR group. We walked for three days before we came across a kraal headman who could tell us where the MNR were based. It was another day's walk to our north. The headman gave us some local *aguadente* firewater, distilled from bananas, in a very old glass Coca-Cola bottle. It was extremely strong but he drank it like lemonade. After thanking the headman and giving him some cheap printed cotton cloth, we set off up a steep escarpment in the direction of the MNR base.

The escarpment was nearly vertical as we got near the top and progress was slow. We arrived in the MNR camp in the late afternoon of our fourth day of walking. There were no sentries posted which was unusual. This was a typical terrorist base camp, with trenches dug on the perimeter and thatched shelters for the troops to live in. We found one of the commanders and he showed us to Luke's living area. Luke told one of his bodyguards to show us to the 'visitors' quarters' which were thatched shelters with raised sleeping areas not too far away.

I spoke to Luke first and found him to be very quiet, withdrawn and unhappy. He was in a bunker dug for his protection within a network of trenches. He obviously felt that the Rhodesians had let him down and that he was being left to 'wither on the vine'. At that point, Captain Steyn arrived and told me to go. He was rude and abrupt. I thought that if he adopted that attitude with the MNR, they would dig their heels in and not cooperate. Clearly the Captain felt he had the whip hand.

I don't know what happened during his meeting with Luke but I can guess. Luke was probably told that his new master was now the South African government and that the MNR base in Udzi was to move shortly, with all personnel and the radio transmitter to South Africa. After the meeting, Luke looked even unhappier.

While the meeting was going on, I took the opportunity to speak to some of the MNR faces I remembered from my previous trip. I bumped into the MNR 'secretary' who kept the records of the group. He was either drunk or doped or both and had lost a lot of body weight since I last saw him. Then I saw Luke's radio operator. He was dirty, which was very unlike him. It seemed to me that discipline was failing and that the organization was on the verge of crumbling.

Next morning two Puma helicopters arrived to take us home. Luke saw us off but did not say anything. Each chopper had long-range fuel tanks inside which left little room for the helicopter technician and the three passengers. However, we piled our kit on top of the tanks and squeezed our bodies in between the fuel tanks. The choppers lifted off in a whirl of dust and leaves, creating a mini dust storm. Nobody on the ground waved at us which was not normal. Africans are usually a happy lot and the sight of a helicopter is normally an excuse for singing, dancing and merry-making.

Looking out of the window, I could see that the Puma was taking the same route out that we had used to walk in. I timed the flight and it was exactly twenty minutes to the bush camp in Rhodesia. It had taken us four days to walk in and twenty minutes to chopper out.

The chopper carrying Trooper J and me landed while the other helicopter circled overhead. We jumped out and the Puma lifted off immediately, flying south to South Africa. After a brief chat with the troop commander, I had a quick wash while the camp was being packed up and we drove directly back to Kabrit barracks in Salisbury.

In March that year I got married. The happy day was Friday, March 21 1980. My wife and I were married by the Salisbury District Commissioner, some of the last people to be married by him. He was replaced by a black DC the following Friday. The morning after our marriage we left our apartment early and drove to Kabrit barracks. My wife dropped me at the wooden garden shed that was my sergeant's accommodation and then went home. I got some kit together and waited for the other two guys who would be coming with me.

A few days previously, the Commanding Officer SAS had briefed me and two others on a mission involving the MNR. We met up at about 10 o'clock that morning and put our kit on the 2.5 Mercedes Unimog that was to take us to Udzi and the MNR camp. We arrived in Udzi about four hours later and went into the house used by the white staff. We found things had changed.

MNR commanders.

The house was almost empty and we were greeted by a soldier who used to be a medic in the SAS and was now working for Special Branch. He told us to wait for an SB fellow who would be along shortly. The SB man turned up much later in his Ford Impala motorcar. He smelled of drink and told us to put our kit in his car. He took us off to the Udzi motel where he would brief us and where we would spend the night. At the motel we booked in and ordered some drinks. Clearly the SB man liked a few drinks now and again. We were told we would be leaving next morning and would be driving trucks with MNR kit and personnel to their new camp near Phalaborwa in South Africa.

"Which one of you chaps is the mechanic?" he asked.

We laughed. He seemed annoyed that he had specifically requested a mechanic and one had not been supplied.

We spent the day at the motel and had a few drinks in the bar that night. The bar was packed with local farmers and the mood was merry. This was the week before Robert Mugabe took power. Was it like this in Hitler's bunker just before the Russians closed in, I wondered?

MOZAMBIQUE NATIONAL RESISTANCE 175

One local man at the pub offered me a farm. He owned five farms in the area and three were idle, so he was looking to put managers on them. I told him I was from west London and what I knew about farming was dangerous. He was very insistent that I should take him up on his offer. I said I would think about it. I am still thinking!

Next day, our SB man told us that the move had been delayed until Monday morning, so we waited around at the motel again. On Monday morning we were picked up and off we went to the MNR camp. It was a camp no longer, the place was entirely empty. Everything had been loaded onto trucks and a Crocodile armoured personnel carrier, constructed on an Isuzu 7-ton chassis. However, one of the Bedford trucks would not start. After bleeding the air out of the fuel system, we got it started and the convoy, including the Impala motorcar was on the road.

In my truck I had two MNR guys who ran the Radio Free Mozambique, the voice of the resistance. Our truck held their transmitter which they were going to erect at the new camp in South Africa. It took two days to reach the border at Beitbridge due to breakdowns. We refuelled at military camps on the way. At Beitbridge our personal weapons, FN rifles, had to be placed with the British South Africa Police station for safekeeping before we crossed the border. This was a joke because we were carrying cases full of weapons in the trucks. Again, one of the trucks was getting air into the system and it had to be bled free of air. The SB fellow smoothed our way through the border posts and we entered South Africa.

Our first stop was the Defence Force camp in Pietersburg where we refuelled the trucks and got a mechanic to look at the problem vehicles. Here we were met by some South African Defence Force drivers. We were under the impression that we would be taking the vehicles on to the new camp located inside the Kruger National Park near Phalaborwa in the Eastern Transvaal. The South Africans thought differently and commandeered the vehicles.

The SB chap had business in Pretoria, so we all climbed into his car and headed for the capital.

It was at this stage that we three soldiers got to know our SB guy better. His bag of personal kit would make clinking noises and from here on we noticed he would start drinking early in the morning. One morning he got as far as 10 o'clock before having a drink. After Pretoria, we headed back for Salisbury and stayed overnight at Pietersburg and Beitbridge for no other reason than to give the SB guy a chance to do some more drinking at company expense. The man was a liability. Why he was trusted, I will never know.

By the 1990s, the MNR, or Renamo as the organization was referred to by the South Africans, were more bandits than freedom fighters. However, one must give credit to Afonso for keeping the organization together through the bad times and achieving the aim of fighting his way to the negotiating table and emerging as a legitimate political party. Afonso and Renamo are now in government in Mozambique, Frelimo has ditched its radical communist ideology and the country is thriving.

11
End of an era

By early 1980, it was obvious that the game for the whites in Rhodesia was drawing to a close. We had had a good innings but the white population was declining due to emigration. The economy was winding down and the cost of the war was spiralling out of control. There was simply not enough money to continue the war.

The Lancaster House talks in London were not going well; the Rhodesians were in a position where they had to agree to elections on the basis of one-man, one-vote. The terrorist forces of Robert Mugabe's ZANLA and those of Joshua Nkomo's ZIPRA were brought out of the bush into holding camps and the Rhodesian security forces were moved back to barracks. A British monitoring force from the army and various regional police forces was drafted in to secure the terrorist holding camps and oversee the election process. As the election drew nearer, the Rhodesians formed contingency plans to be put in place should the election not go our way. It was planned that the Rhodesian Light Infantry and the Rhodesia Regiment would neutralize various terrorist holding camps and the SAS would neutralize Robert Mugabe and his entourage at their accommodation in a hostel at the University of Rhodesia. I am not sure what the Selous Scouts were going to do nor do I remember what plans were made regarding Joshua Nkomo, although he was seen as the lesser of the two liberation evils—and that in spite of his gloating over the downing of the two Viscounts.

In the days running up to the election, the SAS mobilized every man it had. All Territorial Force members were called up and even guys who had failed a selection course and were waiting for the next one were pressed into service. We had fewer than 100 operational men by scraping the very bottom of the barrel.

The SAS 2 i/c attended a briefing at Army HQ regarding the likely outcome of the election and passed this information on to the entire regiment in the cinema at Kabrit barracks one afternoon. His briefing indicated that our man, Prime Minister Bishop Abel Muzorewa of the moderate United African National Council (UANC), would scrape in with a small majority. I don't think many of us at the briefing believed this. We all knew that thousands of terrorists were still in the bush and were actively intimidating the local population in the Tribal Trust Lands. We were correct: there was massive intimidation and the voting split down tribal lines with the Matabele voting for Joshua Nkomo and the Mashona for Robert Mugabe. No surprise there then.

It was time to put the Alternative Plan into effect.

A model of the hostel used by Robert Mugabe was made in the camp cinema and the regiment was briefed on the plan of attack. The plan was simple: early one morning the regiment would secure the area around the hostel, supported by one Soviet-built T-54 tank and one Eland 90 armoured car. A number of tanks, manufactured in Russia, had been on the way to Uganda by cargo vessel when it had berthed in Durban and the cargo was confiscated by the South Africans. These tanks were then supplied to Rhodesia. The armoured cars were a French design, locally manufactured in South Africa, and carried an effective 90mm gun. After receiving the code word from Army HQ, the building would be razed to the ground by the tank, the armoured car and by our own 106mm recoilless rifle anti-tank guns. The ruins would be cleared by teams in body armour and gas masks and any persons fleeing across the open ground on three sides of the hostel would be neutralized by the stop groups. Nothing very clever in this plan, but it was simple and minimized any risk to the attackers. I commanded a stop group in the *vlei*, a flat open area, on the one side of the hostel with orders to kill anything attempting to cross the *vlei*.

The regiment moved out of Kabrit barracks to a forming-up point in a side street near the university. As dawn broke, we waited for the code word. It never came. I recall standing next to the truck when the order came to return to camp. I felt utterly despondent, sick and empty. That moment was one of the worst I ever experienced.

It was the end of an era. We all felt badly let down.

Two weeks later, another plan to kill Mugabe was carried out. Specific intelligence indicated that Mugabe would be flying in to the airfield at Fort Victoria on a specific day at a specific time. Several TM46 anti-tank mines were fixed to the roof of a culvert under a road near the airfield using the tried and trusted super-glue method. The mines were rigged for remote detonation from a location in a clump of nearby bushes. The charges detonated a fraction of a second too late. Mugabe crossed the culvert momentarily before detonation.

It was close but not close enough.

The SADF made offers to the Rhodesian SAS to come and join their operation as a complete unit and form 6 Reconnaissance Commando. About fifty people took advantage of the offer, including me. Some of the volunteers were not 'real' operators; many had crawled out of the woodwork from desk jobs and training depots and had seen little or no service in the war.

6 Recce Cdo did not last very long. Many people left after the first year and most of the rest left a year after that. The SAS Association of Southern Africa was quickly formed with its headquarters initially in Johannesburg. Sadly the ex-member who offered the use of his business premises in Johannesburg, as a meeting place for the monthly reunions, took all the memorabilia then banned anyone from entering the place. The SASASA HQ is now in Durban and the individual is himself banned.

In 1991 the SASASA celebrated the fiftieth anniversary of the founding of the Special Air Service in fine style in Johannesburg. In company with several other people such as Mike Wiltshire, formerly of Parachute Training School in Salisbury, we arranged for fifty static-line parachutes and a DC-3 from the South African Air Force.

The SAS was founded in 1941 by David Stirling in North Africa. Rhodesians had formed C Squadron of 22 SAS Regiment when it was formed in the 1950s. As Rhodesians it was our duty to celebrate the anniversary in the best style we could. Initially, Recce HQ in Pretoria promised to supply the 'chutes but a major there blocked the loan at the very last minute. Mike Wiltshire, a former Rhodesian Parachute Jumping Instructor, was very annoyed, having taken a day off work and organized a truck to collect the equipment. At the very last minute 44 Parachute Brigade stepped into the breach and saved the day by sending a lorry with fifty parachutes. I signed for the 'chutes and signed a waiver that all damage would be made good.

The next problem was an aeroplane.

I went to Pretoria to see the South African Air Force department that authorized the deployment of aeroplanes and met with Colonel Dick Lord, an English-speaking South African. He told me that, although born in South Africa, he had served as a young man in the Royal Navy as a pilot in the Fleet Air Arm. He said he made one parachute jump when he ejected from a jet fighter while on secondment to the US Navy. He stunned me when he asked, "How many aircraft do you want?" I told him one would be enough. He said it would be delivered to a local municipal airfield and we could have it all day.

It was as simple as that.

I had to sign a form in which I promised to make good any damage to the aircraft. The next problem was to get permission to use a local farm as a drop zone. The South African Parachute Association was very helpful and all I had to do was to sign a form guaranteeing third party liability. In addition, a marquee was hired, a pig roast was organized and everything came together. People came from all over the country for the day and we all had a very good time.

Nothing went wrong although Doug Parker broke his toe on landing. There were also several jumpers, Jock Hutton and George Kay, in their 70s who had both jumped in the Second World War. I was worried that having signed so many waivers and indemnities and public liabilities, if anything went wrong I would be in severe trouble. Luckily nothing did go wrong

Not even a single reserve parachute was stolen, which amazed me!

12

Angola, Somalia and Iraq

Angola
At the end of 1992 I became a partner in Para Security in Johannesburg, South Africa. The company was involved in static site guarding and armed response. I joined the company to start the armed-response business and was promised ten per cent of all the profit on this business. Initially, the armed-response department had three response vehicles and eight armed response personnel. Every client had an alarm system in their house and a panic button. In the event of an intruder entering the property, the client would summon one of our armed-response vehicles by pressing the panic alarm. The signal would be received by our control-room operator who would dispatch a vehicle to the property. All response personnel were armed with handguns. It was a fairly profitable business in Johannesburg at that time and we were one of a large number of companies offering armed-response services. I was working a huge number of hours and looking forward to some good profits at the end of the year. When the senior partner bought a Rolls Royce as his company car, I quickly realized that the profits would not be going into my pocket.

When a friend of mine from the Selous Scouts mentioned that he had started an operation in Luanda, Angola, looking after diamond dealers, he told me it was going well and he would soon need some more supervisors. I asked him to keep me in mind. It was not long before I had a phone call asking me when I could start. I finished at Para Security and got my kit ready to go to Angola. I didn't know what I was letting myself in for but the pay was in US dollars and that was all I needed to know. In those days we flew to Luanda from Johannesburg by South African Airways to Swakopmund in Namibia, then by Angola Air to Luanda. The flight to Swakopmund was uneventful but the flight to Luanda was unusual. Angola Air had a policy of selling as many tickets as they could, regardless of how many seats there are on the plane. At Swakopmund I had to fight for a seat on the plane by climbing over the backs of other passengers to get to the check-in counter. It was a long climb but I made it. The aircraft was an Ilyushin passenger jet that had seen better days. The terminal at Luanda airport had also seen better days and nothing worked. The lighting, the air-conditioning and the baggage carousel—nothing worked. The airport had X-ray machines but they didn't work either. Nothing in Angola appeared to work.

On the ride to the accommodation there were potholes in the road that a bus could disappear into. In some areas there was sewage bubbling up through the road and there were piles of garbage on the roadsides. One could see that Luanda had once been a pretty colonial city but in 1993, after decades of war in Angola, first against the Portuguese and then a civil war, the place was crumbling. Our accommodation was on the top floor of the Casa Sportivo, on the Ihlya, a sand spit that runs in an arc out to sea and forms the harbour. In the harbour were a number of sunken ships, an old car ferry that had been turned into a floating hotel and discotheque, a jack-up oil rig and not much else. As a port it had seen better days. I met Vance who introduced me to our employer, a Portuguese Jew whose core business was dealing in raw diamonds but had branched out into other areas where he believed money could be made. Several friends of mine were there already there.

Luanda was a violent town where everybody carried guns and money could buy anything. At night one could watch the tracer bullets on the skyline above the city and listen to the chatter of machine guns. I don't mean just light weapons: one could hear heavy stuff like 23mm anti-aircraft guns as well. There were Jews, Lebanese and Asians involved in any business that would turn a buck. It was usually risky and usually something to with diamonds or currency. De Beers, the international diamond mining business, ran mines in the interior but there were also independent dealers, mostly Jews, who operated in Luanda buying raw stock and transporting it, mainly to Antwerp.

In the interior of the country, riverbeds were dug out by Angolan peasants who searched for rough diamonds in the gravel. When a digger had enough diamonds, he would sit at the edge of a road with his stock on a piece of newspaper until a buyer came along. Typically, a buyer would be an Angolan in a four-wheel-drive pick-up truck with guards armed with AK-47 rifles. He carried large amounts of local currency, Angolan "Kwanzas", and haggled with the digger before striking a bargain. The digger would get enough cash to buy his soap, candles, and anything else he needed. The buyer would return to Luanda with the raw, uncut diamonds, where he would hawk the diamonds around the independent dealers until he got the price he wanted. The digger got his soap and candles, the buyer got US dollars and raw stock was sent around the world.

The year before I arrived, Vance had set up the security at the 'diamond house', a fortified house with high walls, armed guards, steel plates on the doors and windows and a room in the middle of the property with no outside walls. It had a concrete floor and roof, but no windows. It contained just a table, a safe and a white light suspended from the ceiling. This was the diamond room where stock was sorted into piles of diamonds of differing quality and size, and where cash and stock was kept. Once a month the diamond sorters would put Vaseline on their hands and go over the entire floor picking up diamonds. Diamonds stick to grease and nothing else.

As Luanda became more violent and lawless in the early 1990s, other independent dealers wanted this level of protection, so our security business expanded. The company was given a name, Angolanos Seguranza Limitada. Soon the company provided the security for all seven independent Jewish diamond dealers' houses.

Air France flew into Luanda twice a week with a Boeing 747 from Paris. It was usually less than half full, but I guess the French were willing to pay to retain their footprint in that part of Africa. In early 1993, one night as the Jumbo from Paris landed, a 'skirmish line' of Angolan bandits, armed with AK-47s, crossed the runway out of the darkness and robbed everybody on the plane. Angolanos Seguranza was given the contract to provide two pick-ups with armed men twice a week to guard the Air France Jumbo. Our pick-up trucks would follow the aircraft down the runway as it landed and provided a perimeter of armed men while it was on the ground being refuelled. This took about three hours. On board were two French security guards, armed with handguns, who searched everybody and their baggage before they boarded the plane. When the plane was refuelled our trucks would follow the Jumbo along the runway until it took off. We also provided armed guards for the residences of the four Air France expatriate employees.

Word got around that Angolanos Seguranza Limitada provided reliable armed security. Soon our clients included the Lebanese who ran warehouses down by the docks selling clothes, white goods and electrical goods. Then we started doing cash-in-transit. Retailers, both Asian and Lebanese, wanted a safe place for their cash at night. We began by using a small 4x4 vehicle for the bags of local currency and a pick-up truck for the guards but after a while the volumes of cash became so great we needed a bigger vehicle. We bought all our AK rifles through an Angolan 'fixer' for US$50 each, a bit steep but he always got us what we wanted. We asked this guy to get us a bigger truck.

Cash in transit, at Box Gafar, the cigarette seller, Luanda, 1993.

Next morning he drove up to Casa Sportivo in a Soviet-made six-wheeled BTR 152 armoured personnel carrier. He wanted $150 for it. Since it was probably stolen it from the Angolan Army, this might have caused problems so we said no. Instead, we bought two left-hand-drive 4x4 vehicles specially imported from Europe. One had German plates and the other Swiss plates. I guess they might have been stolen as well.

Initially our guards were dressed in civilian clothes, but these gave us a rag-tag appearance, so I found a clothing manufacturer in Luanda and got a quote on 200 shirts and 200 trousers. Then I had to order more because the business was expanding. This made the guards look infinitely smarter and made them act smarter too. It was a good investment, because it was advertising. Soon we were doing security for retail shops and for a UN housing complex.

In central Luanda we went from twelve to 250 guards in two months. I had to learn Portuguese quickly and it was a fast learning curve. I had two guards who could speak English and one who could write as well. The reader/writer became the secretary and the other the sergeant-major.

One of the contracts we picked up was at the depot of a Portuguese engineering contractor, handling reinforced concrete work. He had about 100 Portuguese expats living there in a compound. The depot was out of Luanda on the coast road north. On the way we drove past the prison, a shabby,

Guards on parade in Luanda before the new uniforms arrived, 1993.

Guards with new uniforms at the new parade area, Luanda, 1993.

dilapidated old fort, where several mercenaries from the Angolan civil war of the '70s were being held. The unlucky ones, including Costas 'Colonel Callan' Georgio, had been executed near here. Anyone sentenced to life or any term of imprisonment, for that matter, was quite unfortunate. Years later I met an English guy with a limp who had been caught by the Angolans with Georgio and who had been sentenced to life. He was released after eight years in solitary confinement. I asked him if he'd ever felt lonely. "I was never alone; I always had Jesus," was his response.

One day on the Ihlya, I saw a square parachute landing on the beach close to a nearby hotel. I drove down and had a few words with the parachutist. His name was Tenente Francisco, a light-skinned mulatto and an officer in the Angolan Army. The hotel manager paid him to jump onto the beach to amuse the guests. He used an Angolan Air Force Alouette III helicopter which was also paid for by the hotel. The next day, I accompanied him to the air force base opposite the civilian airport and saw the *paraquedista* or paratroop operation, which had a few Russian square civilian parachutes, a rigger and a handful of people and not much else. The rigger was packing parachutes by dragging them across a raw concrete floor on a veranda. As a parachute rigger he was dangerous. Most of the rigs looked in poor condition and by European or American standards would have been condemned. Francisco told me about an operation he had done recently where he had jumped at night into an area the military wanted to use as a landing zone for a helicopter-borne assault. He jumped alone using a Russian sport square parachute and a small voice radio. When the helicopters arrived next morning, he talked them in using the radio. He had balls but little training.

Francisco introduced me to Capitão Diamante, another light-skinned Angolan, and the leader of the six paratroopers in the team. They used to have more, including two women. I inquired where the ladies were and was told that they had drowned jumping when they had drifted out to sea after jumping on the Ihlya.

The team was going to do a jump into Luanda that afternoon into a children's birthday party and I was given permission to ride in the helicopter. We emplaned in a very old Soviet Mi-8 helicopter once used by Aeroflot, judging by the old paint scheme. We climbed in and I sat down in a canvas seat. I could not do up the lap strap as the buckle had corroded. The pilot, a very black Angolan, climbed in and immediately started up the engine without doing the usual walk around most pilots do, kicking the tyres and such. The

Train Hard, Fight Easy. Angolan Air Force Parachute School, Luanda 1993.

blades rotated slowly and the aircraft rocked from side to side more than any other helicopter I have ever been in, before or since. The paratroopers climbed in. Only one had an altimeter and another had a helmet; the rest had neither. It appears they took it in turns wearing the helmet and using the altimeter. At about 5,000 feet over Luanda, the helicopter started on its jump run. The guy with the altimeter did the 'spot' out of the door, shouted to the pilot and the pilot made some heavy adjustments. The altimeter man jumped first. Everybody followed in a leisurely manner, one by one. When the altimeter man deployed his parachute so did everybody else. Amazingly, they all landed safely in a very narrow street. I was relieved when the helicopter landed.

A chum of mine handled the UN housing-complex security in a compound of fully furnished and prefabricated villas, enclosed by a tall fence and with a guardhouse and boom at the entry point. His guards did twenty-four-hour shifts. One Sunday night an unoccupied villa was emptied of everything moveable. The UN complained in the morning to my friend, a straightforward and uncomplicated Australian. He suspected the guards. He locked himself in a room with the guard commander and beat the fellow until he confessed. The guard commander complained to the police who dropped the charges when they received a hefty bribe. My friend was lucky to get out of that one.

Some De Beers people came to the Casa Sportiva one day to see our boss, wanting him to join their organization. Our boss said to me, "I told them they could join me instead." This turned out to be a bad business decision. My mother was taken ill in late 1993, so I had to leave Angola. A week after I'd left Luanda, the Casa Sportiva was, one morning, surrounded by armed police and all the expat employees were taken off to a safe house before being deported. An Angolan police colonel became the boss and the company was 'Angolanized'. Rumour has it that De Beers paid the Angolan government $50 million to close down all the independent dealers in Luanda.

Somalia

On leaving Angola and returning to the UK, I needed some work quickly. I was contacted by a friend who told me a security company in London needed somebody with African experience for a UN job they were bidding for in Somalia. I went along for a chat and watched them put together a proposal for a UN job training Somalian security guards. It was an awful proposal but the partners seemed satisfied with it and asked me to go to Somalia with one of the them to submit the proposal. After a day in Nairobi, I flew by United Nations C-130 aircraft to Mogadishu where we transferred to a UN Mi-8 helicopter for the short hop to the main UN base. No one there travelled by road unless forced to do so. At that time the UN operation in Somalia was run by Americans with lower-level posts filled by other nationalities. All the jobs involving cash, resources, assets or decision-making were filled by Americans. They appeared to be mostly young graduates with limited experience of Africa, the kind of people who achieved little with their meaningless and endless meetings in which they revelled.

The training contract went to an American company. However, I came away with a six-month contract as security manager on a UN-funded road-building project in Tanzania. It was possibly the worst security job I have ever had: the Italian foremen and supervisors stole more than the local crooks.

Iraq

I was in the bath one day in June 2003 when I had a phone call from a friend in Bristol. A friend of his in Dubai needed some guys for a security job in Iraq. There were no other details available so I should have smelled a rat.

Iraq had been invaded in April of that year and I knew there were guarding contracts being awarded, so I packed my kit for a site guarding job and flew out to Bahrain where I spent the night and then on to Kuwait. In Kuwait we were met by a tall, slim fellow, aged about thirty, with an accent I couldn't place. He was European or Mediterranean, with an American accent. He told us that we were working for him now, not the guy in Dubai, and that he was working for an international security company in Kuwait, that our contracts were on the way, more security personnel were due to arrive and that we would be armed once we entered Iraq. Things seemed fine at this stage. However, hints of doubt were beginning to emerge. Suddenly I had become a sub-contractor to a sub-contractor to another sub-contractor to the employer.

Next day, we entered Iraq by car and drove straight to a hotel in Basra where a friend of his was staying. Basra was quiet and there were no security problems at the time. Here we overnighted before driving two American 4x4 cars north to Baghdad the next morning. I was given a Soviet Tokarev pistol with one magazine and seven rounds of ammunition. I was told more weapons would soon be forthcoming. We passed lines of abandoned Iraqi armoured vehicles and signs of airstrikes in many places. However, the concrete motorways were fairly good and we made decent time. In Baghdad we stayed at a safe house and continued next day to Kirkuk in the north, on the edge of Kurdistan. We bought fuel at the side of the road from hawkers selling petrol in plastic containers. Here we collected five clients, all academics, employed by a non-profit civil-governance foundation based in North Virginia that works with governments, municipalities and private organizations.

At Kirkuk we went to a house near the air base that was run by Kellogg Brown & Root (KBR). Our 'boss' departed almost immediately, leaving another British guy and me to look after the five clients and two vehicles, and armed with two untested handguns and a handful of bullets. Our sole means of communication was one satellite phone. We stayed in Kirkuk for a few days at the house which was protected by Ghurkas employed by a London-based security company. Every day we took the academics to meetings in Mosul, Erbil, Sulimaniya and around Kirkuk. They dealt with women's groups, religious groups, lawyers and the like.

Also in the house were two Kurdish-Americans. Both had been born in Kurdistan and had moved to the USA as infants. One of them had bad toothache and so one day we transported him to the American base at Mosul for treatment. On the way we chatted. He told me that he had been contacted at his home in New Jersey by US government people a year before the invasion of Iraq in April 2003. Several months before the invasion he had been taken to Kuwait and while the invasion was in progress he had been "flown over the top into Kurdistan to talk to Kurdish people". It appears that preparations for war had been made well over a year before we, in the UK, were being prepared for it by the Blair regime.

Our client decided to relocate us all to an hotel outside Erbil on the road to Salah-ud-Din. The house we had vacated was hit by an RPG-7 rocket that night.

On arrival at the hotel, we settled in and I received a call from the client to go and see him. A Kurd from Erbil had arrived at the hotel and asked for our client by name. He carried a message; "Come to see my boss immediately." The client said no and the Kurd became agitated. He explained that his boss was a "big man" and would be very insulted. An agreement was reached whereby our client, escorted by me, would travel into Erbil later that afternoon to visit the 'big man'. We went in one car which I drove and followed the directions we had been given. We turned off just before the big mosque and went behind a dress shop into a courtyard. Several Peshmergas, local militia, dressed in baggy pants and carrying AK-47 rifles, surrounded our car. Trying not to look too worried, I got out of the car and opened the door for the client. We were taken into a very large office where we were welcomed by the 'big man' who gave us his business card. He spoke excellent English and explained that he was a Kurd, had lived in London and could call on 20,000 Peshmerga soldiers if he needed them. He appeared to know all about the client and said he wanted to help if he could. The client explained he needed six vehicles and drivers and some security guards, as well as better weapons for me and my colleague. After tea was served, we made excuses to leave and returned to the hotel.

Next morning the vehicles and drivers arrived. The client's people split into two groups; one went to Erbil and the other to Mosul. In the next few days we moved base to an hotel in the centre of Erbil. The client's people only worked a five-day week but my colleague and I were on the go all the time—every day we became extremely tired. One day the client's boss visited from Baghdad in a six-vehicle motor convoy and left four vehicles with us. Local drivers were hired. New weapons did not appear, so the client gave us $200 each; one of our drivers who lived in Erbil bought two folding-butt AK-47s with magazines and ammunition. Now we were in business but we still did not have the extra manpower and contracts that had been promised … and our pay was late. Several satphone calls to our 'boss' in Baghdad gave us no satisfaction and my colleague spoke of walking off the job. I was more inclined to wait until we had been paid and then decide what to do.

One Sunday morning I escorted one of our female clients, an Iraqi-born American, to the top of the Citadel in Erbil. This is a man-made hill, several hundred feet high, that has been inhabited for several thousand years. It was like going back into time: things have not changed up there for millennia. Erbil also has a Christian suburb, Ankawa, where one can buy alcohol and has a small restaurant called The Edge Club where one can buy a sort of South African *boerewors* sausage. It was not exactly *boerewors* but it was close. Mosul is also fascinating and one can see the remains of the city of Nineveh. It has Christian churches and under Saddam Hussein there was freedom of worship. Sulimaniyah is another fascinating place with ancient mosques and *suqs*, or markets, to wander around in.

On one trip to Kirkuk I bumped into an old friend from my Angola days who was working with some former South African Reconnaissance Commandos. I saw him again on another trip to Sulimaniyah. They were bodyguarding an American VIP.

While on a trip to Baghdad, my colleague walked off the job. None of the promises made by our 'boss' had materialized in terms of contracts, pay, weapons and manpower. My colleague went to work for a London-based company he had previously worked for. However, more manpower arrived in Mosul in the form of an ex-French navy guy and two ex-Legionnaires who were Sicilian brothers from Palermo. When two more of their ex-Legionnaire friends arrived in Mosul things got worse. They were bringing women into the hotel and then there were two cases of theft from the clients. I spoke to the client and explained that I did not trust the others, especially the Sicilians, and would be making plans to leave as soon as I had been paid.

On a trip to Baghdad I spoke to the client's chief and learned there were plans in place to cancel the current security contract. Sure enough, the security contract was cancelled shortly afterwards.

I left and returned to the UK and 'phoned around looking for work. I quickly got two interviews on the same day. A job offer came soon after and I packed my kit and headed off to the airport to catch a flight to Kuwait. From Kuwait I took a US Air Force C-130 to Baghdad and after a long wait, was picked up by a company vehicle and went to their camp. Like most camps in Iraq, it comprised second-hand portakabins, relocated from a Saudi oil camp a few weeks before. I learned I was to be on the Iraq Currency Exchange programme

(ICE). The company was going to be shipping all the new currency into Iraq and transporting the old Saddam Hussein money to centres for destruction. I met several other ex-Rhodesian Army guys in Baghdad. The next day, two of us were flown by Ilyushin 76, loaded with currency, to Basra.

The ICE contract had been put together at short notice. Custer Battles, a notorious American company was contracted to erect the three camps at Basra, Baghdad and Mosul and to supply all the logistics including food, water, electricity and everything else required to sustain life. Each camp contained more than 120 men. At Basra we had 100 Fijians and twenty ex-pats from UK, Australia, Ireland, America and Poland Most of the manpower came from the 2nd Battalion the Fiji Regiment. Some were good guys and some were just plain lazy. We had some excellent welders, vehicle fitters and carpenters among them. Their officers were quick to see that what they were being paid by the company was not what was being charged out for their services. So, several Fijian officers approached the client directly, requesting employment. They were promptly fired.

Vehicles arrived at Basra. Within a few days we had forty-seven vehicles, including new Toyota Hilux pick-ups and Land Cruisers, and a lot of very old Iraqi trucks, most of which were dangerous. Custer Battles were paid to supply new portakabins, new trucks, new diesel generators and a daily allowance of $56 per man for food. Only the Toyotas were new. The caterer told me that he was not allowed to spend more than $5 per man per day on food. The food was awful. The Basra camp was not completed until one week after the ICE programme was completed. Custer Battles management should be shot. But they weren't the only scammers on the site.

Several people in the organization were fired and given ten minutes to clear their desks for various crimes, mainly fraud. I was the motor transport officer for most of my stay at Basra but I also went out on convoys delivering money. I had several Filipino tradesmen to help in keeping the vehicles on the road and these men were absolutely first-class. A less impressive person was an ex-cop from America who was also our medic. His standard of weapon training was very low and I watched him have a negligent discharge (ND) on a trip to Basra port. He would sling his M16 rifle over his shoulder with a round in the breech and the safety catch off. He would insist on getting out of his vehicle and talking to Iraqi boys. A boy once slipped behind him and pulled the trigger of his rifle. I understand he had four ND's in two years in Iraq.

Another ND I witnessed was in the barrack one night when I watched

Baghdad, Iraq, June 2003. The author on throne in Saddam Hussein's palace.

a former Black Watch captain playing with his Beretta pistol. It was plain he had little pistol experience. He was taking a full magazine off, cocking, squeezing the trigger, then magazine on, then mag off, cock and squeeze and so on until it went bang. He shot a hole in the wall opposite his bed. Nobody said anything but somebody put a target over the hole and made a hole in the middle. This was worse than saying something. The fine for a negligent discharge was a day's pay.

Nobody from the ICE contract was killed in my time at Basra although we lost one Fijian from a heart attack and three had to be sent home with heart conditions and hypertension. After the age of forty, Fijians appear to be prone to such conditions. The only ex-pats we lost were two Australians who were both fired.

After Basra I was posted to Baghdad to look after the Iraqi ambassador to the USA who was in town for meetings. She was a very nice lady and it wasn't a bad fortnight. Following Baghdad, I went to Mosul to join Operation North Star, a contract escorting convoys from the Turkish border to a point about 120 kilometres south of Mosul, where we handed over to US Army convoy escorts. The convoys comprised up to 100 trucks, carrying everything from fuel to portakabins to food. North Star consisted of 120 men and eighteen vehicles split into six 'platoons'. The platoon I commanded had three vehicles and fifteen men. I rode in a Toyota Land Cruiser; the other two vehicles were Toyota Hi-Lux pick-ups. All doors were removed except for the drivers' doors which had plate steel behind them. The pick-ups had post-mounted M240 belt-fed machine guns. Every shooter, or rifleman, had an M16 rifle or an M249 Minimi machine gun. My 2 i/c was Eugene Pomeroy. We worked out of Al Qurayah airfield, known as Q-West, about eighty kilometres south of Mosul, where we lived in the old ICE camp. There were three three platoons stationed at Q-West, with another three working out of Saddam Hussein's old palace in Mosul.

Days could be very long. In the winter we often experienced sub-zero temperatures in the mountains of Kurdistan, whereas on the plains in summer, midday temperatures would peak at about 50° centigrade. We would often depart Q-West before dawn, drive north to Mosul then on to the Turkish border, collecting the vehicles once they were ready and setting off for the drop-off point. Stops would be made if the convoy was too strung out. We might not get back to Q-West until dark.

We were officially known as G Company, Stryker Brigade, Task Force Olympia. Strykers were high-tech eight-wheeled armoured personnel carriers used by the US Army. These were too high-tech for Iraq and were more suitable for use in urban areas than in a counter-insurgency role. They had cameras mounted on the roof for observation but these were vulnerable to direct fire from high-rise apartment blocks. Even though a Stryker could drive if it lost a wheel on each side, it was easy to burn all the tyres using homemade napalm made from soap and petrol. These "Improvised Explosive Devices" were left lying in a gutter surrounded by rubbish or cast into cement like a kerbstone.

At night the insurgents would prise out kerbstones and replace them with an Improvised Explosive Device's. These IEDs were often initiated by a mobile telephone or an automatic door closer or model aeroplane radio-control system. The initiator, known as a 'dicker', would have the target vehicle in sight and operate the system when the target reached a marker such as a lamppost or a pile of rocks. The IED could be a pipe bomb, an artillery shell or a mortar bomb placed in a plastic bag, inside a lamppost or in a kerbstone. Gas cylinders were also filled with explosive and mortar bombs were dug into roadside embankments. In 2005 we witnessed our first pressure-operated IED which killed one of our Ghurkas and badly wounded another. This pressure operated device might have been two saw-blades inside a car tyres' inner tube.

As protection from electronic devices, each platoon had an electronic counter-measures (ECM) system fitted to the front vehicle. This was a black box with an antenna on the vehicle roof. The antenna emits a high amount of radio-frequency energy over a short radius and blocks radio communications within that area. The disadvantage is that it has a limited effective radius and only the front vehicle and the vehicle behind it are protected while the ECM is in operation. The other problem is that long-distance communication with the HF radio is blocked out when the ECM is in use.

In 2005 one of our ex-pats was killed in Mosul when a single bullet went through his vehicle windscreen. The driver panicked and sped off without checking the vehicles behind him. These vehicles then hit an effective IED which punctured two tyres on each pick-up truck. The 2 i/c, an Australian, handled the situation extremely well. As usual with IEDs, the HF radio immediately became unserviceable due to the blast damage to the automatic tuner on the front of the vehicle, so he had no communications with base and had to live on his wits. On wheel rims he drove his vehicles out of the killing zone and went into all-round defence in a safe area. The punctured tyres were removed and he and his Ghurkas took them across the road to a tyre shop. He got back on the road and returned to base.

One day in June 2004, Eugene and I were involved in an incident returning to Q-West from Mosul. I was in the lead, our Ghurka platoon sergeant was in the middle vehicle and Eugene's pick-up was at the rear. We maintained fifty-metre spacing between vehicles. On exit from a large traffic circle I was blocked by a blue BMW which refused to get out of my way for at least a kilometre. Once past the BMW, I noticed shopkeepers closing up when they should be open; there was also a noticeable lack of people on the streets. The road here had three lanes each way with a centre intersection with some lampposts in the middle. After crossing a traffic intersection, I saw a red flicker reflected in my spectacles. Then I felt a pressure wave and then an enormous bang. Looking behind, I saw our second vehicle and behind that a wall of dust rising into the sky. I thought Eugene had "bought the farm."

I went straight into the standard operating procedures (SOPs) I had taught the men. I drove on for 200 metres and stopped. A few of our men had scratches from shrapnel but nothing serious. I put them into all-round defence and selected three men to accompany me back to where Eugene should have been. The dust was dissipating but there was no sign of Eugene or his pick-up truck. We moved along the road in extended line. A few rounds popped about, emanating from some high-rise flats on the opposite side of the road. Fire was returned. On reaching the intersection, I found Eugene's pick-up truck off the road, hard up against a tree. The windscreen was totally opaque and pushed inward. The front of the vehicle was covered in shrapnel holes and the two front tyres were flat. Eugene was on the ground next to his front wheel with a thousand-yard stare in his eyes. His Fijian driver was limping around with blood coming out of his boots and waving his AK-47, shouting, "I'm gonna kill somebody." The rear machine gunner had gone over the top of the post-mounted gun and was lying on the pavement. The two men who had been in the rear seats were standing in the road returning some rifle fire that was coming from an alleyway across the street.

I saw a parked car on the opposite side of the street with a head bobbing up and down in the front seat. I figured this was the 'dicker' so I gave a fire-control order to target the parked car.

Using my hand-held radio, I called my car to reverse up to Eugene's wreck, as practised, ready to tow it away. We got Eugene on to his feet and put all the casualties into my car and the platoon sergeant's pick-up. Then more rifle fire started coming in. I called to Eugene to strip out the cab of his vehicle so I could torch it. We were not going to stick around any longer fiddling with a tow rope. I put several rounds into the jerry cans of spare fuel on the back of Eugene's pick-up and to my amazement they immediately burst into flames twenty feet high. It wasn't diesel we were using, but jet fuel JP8. This stuff is basically kerosene and certainly does burn well.

We then took the wounded to the American hospital at the airport. Only Eugene's driver was admitted with the other five being released after treatment. On our return to the company base at the palace, our project manager was very annoyed with me for torching the vehicle. I said sorry. He has never forgiven me.

That IED might have been a 155mm artillery round placed inside a lamppost. The ECM device in my vehicle protected my vehicle and the one behind but Eugene was outside the effective radius of the device.

After this, both Eugene and I started hearing that little voice inside your head telling you to get out of the game while you are still ahead. After a good leave, I returned to Op North Star and became the camp commander at Q-West. Things had become very dangerous and we suffered five deaths and a lot of wounded out of a force of 120 men in one twelve-month period. The guys were calling themselves 'Op Death Star'.

One incident that sticks in my mind happened towards the end of my time in Iraq in 2005 when I was at Q-West in the control room one morning. We had three radios in the control room: one was a High Frequency (HF) for communication with our base in Mosul, another an HF for communication with the Stryker Brigade control room on the other side of the Q-West camp, and a VHF radio for short-distance communications. On one of the HF radios I heard that one of our platoons, travelling cross-country on a shortcut not far from Q-West, had hit an IED and suffered one dead and one badly wounded. They were on their HF radio to our base in Mosul, requesting an immediate casualty evacuation by helicopter. They were told to wait as there were no choppers immediately available. I looked out of the door of our control room and saw two American helicopters coming in to land on the opposite side of the airfield. I got on to our other HF radio and spoke to the Americans in the Stryker Brigade control room, also on the other side of the airfield. We had good relations with these guys and they had always been helpful. I gave them a concise contact situation report: Paragraph A was a broad-brush description of the situation, Paragraph B was location, or 'locstat', of our own people, Paragraph C was a request for casevac. A young lady officer took my radio message very quickly and efficiently. The two choppers I had seen were immediately turned around and they were at the incident site in five minutes or so. The guys on the ground were grateful.

One of my jobs as camp commander was as 'scrounger'. Our boys were always short of ammunition, rifle oil, and so on but we always had plenty of alcohol. When the platoons were passing through Erbil or Dahouk, they always came back with supplies of Scotch and beer. The prices in Kurdistan were very cheap compared to the UK. A bottle of Famous Grouse was about $5. Once I traded a case of Scotch for 1,100 rounds of Browning .50 calibre ammunition. Another time I traded some bottles of Scotch and some beer to get two forty-foot containers moved from Q-West to the palace at Mosul. This Scotch and beer bought me a huge forklift to lift the containers, two trucks and a place in the transport convoy to Mosul.

The American soldier at Q-West in charge of Iraqi tradesmen, such as plumbers, vehicle mechanics and cleaners, was Sergeant Pfeiffer. He was always short of transport to shift people and equipment like piping, fence posts, sandbags and steel plate. His men were vital to the efficient operation of

DEPARTMENT OF THE ARMY
Headquarters, Task Force Olympia
Multinational Brigade-North (MNB-N), Mosul, Iraq
APO AE 09385

REPLY TO
ATTENTION OF:

AFZH-TFO-CG   25 June 2004

MEMORANDUM FOR: Mr. Charlie Andrews, President and CEO, Global Risk Strategies, Ltd., London, England.

SUBJECT: Letter of Appreciation for Mr. Paul French, Global Risk Strategies Ltd.

1. Mr. Paul French performed his duties as a Section Commander from January to June 2004 magnificently, and he has personally made significant contributions to the successes achieved thus far in Northern Iraq.

2. As Section Commander Mr. French was responsible for all aspects of tactical command, training and administration in support of his Section's 28 men comprised of Expatriates, Fijians and Gurkhas. During his command he completed an extraordinary number of humanitarian and relief missions tasked by TFO, and participated in several engagements with Anti-Coalition Forces (ACF). While engaged in combat with the he expertly directed the tactical employment of his Section and inflicted heavy casualties on the enemy.

3. His efforts helped ensure that all taskings assigned by TFO were executed effectively and safely. Among the results of his work were the safe escort of over 30 Million gallons of fuel through northern Iraq, protection and security for the delegation that added Republic of Korea to the coalition, execution of numerous humanitarian assistance missions including assistance to the Governor of Ninewa and escorting experts who established an effective legal system for the Iraqi people.

4. Mr. French's efforts during the last six months have contributed significantly to development of a more secure Iraq. His performance reflects great credit on himself and Global Risk Strategies, ltd.

CARL L. CHAPPELL JR.
COL, GS
Chief of Staff

Letter of appreciation, Chief of Staff Task Force Olympia.

the airfield but his bosses would not give him the necessary resources. I had two broken trucks and two broken buses left over from the Iraqi Currency Exchange Programme days, so in exchange for the loan of one bus and one truck, he fixed all four vehicles. Pfeiffer liked a drink or two and often came to our camp in the evenings to socialize. He got his drinks and the resources to keep the airfield and camp running, whilst we got our vehicles serviced – it was a "win-win" situation.

One of the other jobs we had was the contract to transport and protect the American mortuary people looking for evidence of Saddam Hussein's genocide. The people were required to find a minimum of fifty corpses so that Saddam could be charged with mass murder. Some of these mortuary soldiers were women, based out of Hawaii. One of them had actually travelled to Vietnam and Siberia searching for US military corpses. In Iraq they were working eighty kilometres west of Q-West. Initially, they had started painstakingly, with spades and trowels, but they discovered so many bodies that they had to bring in earthmoving equipment. They dug up hundreds of corpses, all of which were DNA'd and found to be Kurdish. Men had been separated from the women and all were buried in large pits.

I went to the site several times. It was in a bowl in the ground close to a *wadi*, a dry river course. We were not allowed near the diggings and had to stay on the high ground around the site. One day, three of our people went down to the diggings and peeked under the tarpaulin covering one of the mass graves. They came back and said the bodies were well preserved and that even the dresses looked so bright that it was difficult to believe that the corpses had been there for years. Next morning, the young man who had lifted the edge of the tarpaulin was not fit for work. His pal said he had had a bad headache the previous evening and asked me to look in on him and see how he was. I went straight to his room. He was lying in bed, shivering with a fever. I glanced around and saw that his wash-hand basin was coated with blood that he had vomited over the entire basin. I checked his pulse: it was racing and his temperature was high. I went straight across to the American medical centre on the other side of the airfield and spoke to the US Army Special Forces medic who ran the place. I told him about our man, his symptoms and the fact he had been in close proximity to corpses. I told him I thought we might have found evidence of Saddam's weapons of mass destruction (WMD). He said to

Al Hadr ruins, 80 kilometres west of Q-West airfield.

bring the patient over immediately. I did this and packed a small bag for the man who was taken by helicopter to the American military hospital in Mosul. They kept him in there for a week and said he had 'malaria'. I believe he had a viral haemorrhagic infection. Whether or not it was WMD or a virus spread by insects or rats on the corpses, I do not know, but it was certainly not malaria. The patient appeared to make a full recovery after a week or two, but I often wonder if he suffered long term effects. In my experience, and I've had malaria three times, it does not present suddenly and vomiting so much blood that it floods a wash basin is not one of the symptoms.

Near the mass graves was the site of Al Hadr, an ancient city built by the Assyrians, then occupied by the Greeks and finally by the Romans. Only a small area has been uncovered so far and it reminded me very much of ancient Jordanian ruins. But two years in Iraq was enough. The voices telling me to get out while I was still ahead of the game and could enjoy my money were getting louder. Other friends did not get out while they were ahead and I have been to their funerals.

Appendix
Warning signs

When someone decides to attack you or your convoy of vehicles, either on or off the road, he does leave warning signs, in the same way that someone walking across a field will leave spoor and signs. The signs might not glare out like neon-lit billboards; they might only be very small and only apparent after you have passed them by. The following warning signs are what I have learned to look out for. They are not an exhaustive list and they are not SOPs.

Body language
- When driving through a built-up area, watch the local population. Try and make eye-contact with them.
- If kids are playing in the street and they wave at you, this is a good sign.
- If adults avert your gaze and hurry indoors, this is a bad sign.
- If the streets are deserted when there should be people about, this is a very bad sign.

The vehicle that won't get out of your way
- If a vehicle pulls out in front of you and won't let you get past, this is a bad sign.
- If the same vehicle moves from lane to lane as you try to pass, this is a very bad sign.
- If the same vehicle suddenly pulls over to let you pass, this is a very, very bad sign.
- If the road ahead is then empty of traffic when there should be some traffic, then this is an extremely bad sign.
- This vehicle is a 'blocker'. He is giving his chums down the road time to prepare for an attack. You have been 'spotted' and are about to be "dicked."
- DO A 180° TURN AND USE A DIFFERENT ROUTE!

Shops closing
- Local people in third-world countries know when an 'incident' is about to occur. They know their own villages and towns and know when something out of the ordinary is about to happen.
- If shops are closing when they should be open, then this is a very bad sign.
- If shopkeepers are pulling their stock inside or the roller shutters are being pulled down as you drive past, then this is a warning for you to consider taking your alternative route with immediate effect.
- You have been 'spotted' and the 'dicker' is organizing a welcome for you just a little way down the road.

Traffic density
- Speed and mobility are your best defences.
- Very heavy traffic is bad because it means you might have to stop unless you can find a way around it. When you are stationary you are a target.
- Medium-density traffic is preferable because you can stay mobile and if the locals are out on the streets then it is safe for them and hopefully safe for you.
- Very low-density traffic: when traffic densities should be higher is a very bad sign. It means the locals know it's not safe to be out on the street. This is a warning sign for you to consider taking your alternative route. You may have been 'spotted' and the 'dicker' may have his finger on the button.

Off-road obstacle crossing
- If you have spotted any warning signs and the local terrain is suitable, you might want to consider leaving your planned route and going off-road. Just be aware that the 'dicker' is a clever little boy and he may have placed warning signs on your route to make you leave the road at a specific point.
- Never travel off-road in another vehicle's tracks, especially when crossing an obstacle such as a dried-up riverbed or a saddle between hills.
- Use obstacle-crossing SOPs and, in particular, look for the following:
    - Spoor, or any marks at ground level e.g. footprints, digging marks
    - Signs, or any marks above ground level e.g. drag marks in grass

- - Shadow impressions in the ground that might only be obvious as shadows
  - Soil textures where soil has been disturbed
  - Bumps and/or altered soil patterns
  - Depressions and/or altered soil patterns
- Don't get into a habit of going off-road at the same place, thereby setting a pattern that might be observed by others.

Unusual items in the road

Look out for the following:
- An oil drum at the side of the road: it might be an IED, so go back or go around, and look for a wire coming out of it.
- A gas canister or two at the side of the road: it might be an IED, so see if you can spot a wire, and go around it or go back.
- Rubbish in the kerb: again, it may be harbouring an IED.
- Kerbstones recently removed: the bad guys like to lever out kerbstones and replace them with mortar rounds or artillery shells which are sometimes cast into the concrete.
- Old cars parked with the bonnets up: could it be a car bomb?
- Old car with one occupant: be suspicious of a junk car with one occupant, but with good tyres (they don't want a puncture on this trip!), trying to drive into your convoy or into your checkpoint: this one *is* a car bomb.